THE HAPPY COUPLES GUIDE TO

SELLING YOUR HOME

BY CHAKIB AND JINAN JABER

PICOLEE
PUBLISHING

THE HAPPY COUPLES GUIDE TO
SELLING YOUR HOME

FIRST PICOLEE PUBLISHING EDITION
MARCH 18, 2020

ISBN: 978-1-951857-01-1

WWW.PICOLEE.COM

Dedicated to our daughter Natalie and son Danny,
without whose patience, support, and love
our tasks would have been much less enjoyable.

CONTENTS

INTRODUCTION

LIFE IS A JOURNEY: SHARING WITH YOU OUR LESSONS LEARNED

Take a good look at your home and your reasons for selling. Are you needing to relocate? Is the house too big or too small for you? Would you prefer being closer to work for a shorter commute? Or did that dream home you've always had your eyes on finally come on the market? It could be one of these reasons or an entirely different one. That doesn't matter. What matters is that you know the reason behind it all. Why do you want to sell?

Ask yourself again, *Do you really want to sell?* If the answer is a definite YES, then you need to be as ready as you can with what comes next. You are about to embark on a journey that can be very exciting, but can also be, in many cases, both physically and emotionally taxing.

Once you do decide to sell your home, and you know the reason(s) why, what's next? It's important to be fully prepared for all that is involved in selling your house so the journey is easier on you. It helps to have a guide to walk you through each step, as well as through the emotional struggles and challenges you might encounter. It'll help to know when each stage in the process will likely occur. That's what *The Happy Couples Guide to Selling Your Home* is all about. It's going to walk you through the steps of selling, preparing you for what might happen along the way. We will also share our own experiences with relocating and buying homes, as well as purchasing over 25 investment properties.

We've learned so much in our journeys through many real estate transactions, and are excited to share our insights with you.

A lot of consideration through these steps should be taken into account as part of your planning process. Maybe it's a *Seller's Market*, meaning you can sell at a high price because there's a shortage of available homes. If your mortgage is still high, the sale might pay it off, allowing you to even realize some profit. That's all well and good, but most likely you will also need to purchase a new home, and prices for another house are likely to be higher, too. Are you making enough profit from yours for it to be worthwhile in the long run? Does the property require a large number of renovations? Should you work with a real estate agent? How should you market your house? What is the best way to negotiate? These are just some high level considerations and questions you will need to ask yourself as you work through the process of selling your home.

We truly hope that our lessons learned and our recommended 10 step process will help you in selling your home faster and for more profit.

This book is purely informational and is not meant to provide legal advice or any guarantees on the sale of your house. If you have any questions, please consult a licensed real estate agent or a real estate lawyer.

Understanding Your Needs and Planning

By understanding your needs early on in the process, you can more effectively make the decisions that are geared to meeting those needs.

You need to develop an understanding of your need to sell. If you write things down and plan, it will help reduce the stress of the decision-making process.

Moving is a major life-changing event that will affect you and your family members. To be fully prepared, you will need to plan every step ahead of time.

By understanding your current and future financial needs, you will be able to make better-educated decisions

You must avoid becoming a motivated Seller—a Seller that needs to sell so badly that they will accept extreme trade-offs in order to close the deal.

In our opinion, 3-4 months of planning are required for the sale of your house, in order to minimize your stress and maximize your returns.

Do not worry about the Yo-Yo Factor and not being able to finalize your decision; leaving your home is a process and it may take time to reach important decisions.

CHAPTER ONE

UNDERSTANDING YOUR NEEDS AND PLANNING

By understanding your needs early on in the process, you can make decisions geared to meeting those needs more effectively.

- It's important to develop an understanding of your needs to sell—if you write things down and plan, it will help reduce the stress of the decision making process.
- Moving is a major life changing event and will affect you and your family members. You need to plan every step ahead of time to be fully prepared.
- By understanding your current and future financial needs, you will be able to make better-educated decisions.
- You must avoid becoming a motivated Seller, meaning a Seller that needs to sell so badly that they will accept extreme trade-offs in order to close the deal.
- In our experience, you need 3-4 months of planning for the sale of your house in order to minimize the stress and maximize your returns.
- Do not worry about the "Yo-Yo Factor" and not being able to finalize your decisions. Leaving your home is a process and it may take time to reach important decisions such as whether you should sell or stay, what your financial needs actually are, what your plans are for the future, whether to hire a real estate agent, marketing strategies, etc.

PLANNING IS KEY

By planning ahead, you can avoid the mistake of having to make decisions in a rush and without being fully informed, possibly "leaving money on the table" and also leaving you with regrets.

LIFE EVENTS

Over the past twenty years, we have moved and sold our home four times. Each time, we had a different reason to sell. In addition, as part of our property investments, we have been involved in many real estate transactions over the years. From being on both the Seller and Buyer side of these transactions, we have developed an in-depth understanding on how to negotiate and/or position our home for sale at the right price and in the right way. There were trials and errors, though. The first time we moved was due to relocating from New York to Virginia. In our move, we placed our New York home up for sale without an understanding of the home prices there. CJ got a good job offer with better salary, and we did not take into account the cost of living or the price of buying a home there, especially since we planned to rent for three months to allow our house in New York to sell. We didn't have time to plan ahead due to the short amount of time available before CJ's job started, so we didn't have the time to plan ahead and fully determine the actual amount we would need in the process of moving and getting settled in our new location. As a result, we became motivated Sellers along the way. We were paying rent in VA and a mortgage in NY while the house was on the market. We couldn't continue holding down the mortgage on our house while trying to move forward, so we ended up just accepting an offer to help stop the bleeding. Since we did not have the budgets or planning to prepare the house for sale, we ended up "leaving money on the table."

The second time we moved, we did much better. We then owned a townhouse, and when Jinan finished college, she got a job with a commute of about an hour each way. We had been in the townhouse for a couple of years, and it was in an "up and coming" area of Virginia. Because of the long commute, we made the decision that if Jinan still liked her job after 4 months of being employed there, we would put our townhouse on the market and get a home that would be closer to her work. We decided it would also be an upgrade from what we currently had.

During those four months, we started getting our home ready for sale in anticipation of this happening. A couple days a week, we would check different neighborhoods we liked. We used online searches to find listings on the market. We did not engage with a real estate agent, however, to avoid pressure and to allow us to plan beforehand. Through our planning ahead, we did find an area that was still priced well, but it came with its own challenges. Unfortunately, we did not have the down payment needed for the new area; we needed to sell our home in order to qualify for a mortgage on the new home. The house that we found had been on the market for only one day. It was a Seller's Market, and we did not have an agent to represent us. We reached out to the listing agent and met with the homeowners. Although it was just the first day of listing, we needed to act fast in seeing it. By doing so, we discovered the Sellers were not in a hurry to sell and needed time to move into a new home. We were able to place an offer to close in 45 days, offering the listing price, as well as other concessions. In addition, we formed a personal connection with the Seller, and we used the same agent to list our property.

This real estate transaction was the first time we needed to negotiate. Through the process, we learned the importance of knowing the Seller's needs, and their reasons for selling. We were clear in what our motives and desires were, too. Because of this, we were able to come to negotiating decisions that were mutually agreeable—a "win-win" solution. Remember, Buyers truly interested in your home will tailor their offers to meet your needs, if possible, especially if you are in a Seller's Market. Helping them understand your own needs, without becoming a Motivated Seller or hindering your negotiating leverage, can also be helpful. Be prepared to answer questions, to know what should and shouldn't be shared, and to keep an open mind through the negotiating steps when it comes to selling your home.

After we had our kids and they started growing, we often debated whether we should move or stay in our home. It was a very tough decision, because we loved the neighborhood, but the house was small and the schools were not top rated. Once we made the decision to move, we planned to do so in 3-4 months and took our time to sell.

Through our own experiences, we have found that people want to sell/move for a wide range of reasons. We have bought properties from folks looking to retire, landlords of income properties, homeowners that have outgrown their home, and those who want to downsize. We have purchased properties from owners who can no longer manage their home or income property, as well as those who want to relocate due to job changes. The list goes on and on.

Whatever your reason for selling your own home, once you've made the decision, it is important to have ample time to plan for the selling process and for being prepared for the steps needed to sell your home. If time is short, however, don't dismay. By understanding the steps provided in this book, you can adjust and/or fast track the process. Either way, you'll be prepared the best way that you can, and preparation reaps success, along with less stress.

UNDERSTANDING YOUR FUTURE DIRECTION

Once you start considering the idea that you would like to sell your house, it is important to understand where you're going next. If you know where you are looking to move, you can begin to explore the prices and availability in housing in that area. If you aren't sure where you want to move, you can begin to compare prices in different areas. Go online for currently listed properties; today you have a wide range of online search engines such as realtor.com and zillow.com. You can narrow your search by State, City/Town, and Price Range. You can even be more detailed and search by square footage, bedroom size, how old the house is, etc. These websites can be a great resource, but not the only one. Here are other ways you can search for your home:

1. If your destination is in the same state, and not too far away, drive through different desired neighborhoods and look for sale signs. Properties for sale by owner will not be listed on realtor.com, but zillow.com typically includes some properties for sale by owner. Also, you may come across a property that has just been listed, but hasn't shown up on the website yet. If you find too many for sale signs in a certain neighborhood, be sure to note that. If you decide to look at any of the homes there, ask the Realtor and/or owner for an explanation as to why so many are selling at this time.

2. If you will be moving farther away, take a vacation and get to know the town; drive some backroads and explore. Be sure to get a sense of how far the house is to the nearest hospital, stores, schools, police and fire stations, etc.

3. Check out the weekly real estate ads in papers for locations you are considering or do online searches as markets tend to shift from week to week.

4. Visit open houses for homes of interest when/if they occur. These would also be advertised in the newspaper or on online sites such as realtor.com or zillow.com. By visiting various houses on the market, you can gather important information. You may discover amenities that could be important to you that you didn't consider beforehand. You will begin to have a clearer understanding of your likes and dislikes. There is always the listing Realtor at these open houses and you can obtain some important information from them. Tell them you are in the early stages of listing your home and buying a new one. Do not let them pressure you. Feel free to take their card and later, once you leave the open house, make notes on the back of it as to whether you felt they were pleasant and helpful.

5. Let it be known to your friends and family that you are thinking of buying. They may know of someone who is selling, or considering selling their home.

UNDERSTANDING YOUR FINANCIAL NEEDS

When you understand your future direction, it becomes important to understand how you will be able to financially make it happen. Your financial needs are driven by a number of variables, which include:

- **Current debt at hand** - You need to know if you can financially afford a new home before you put your current home up for sale. When applying for a mortgage, you will be evaluated for your debt-to-income (DTI), and the ratio will have to be within the lending range. That ratio may vary depending on lender and/or product, but a good rule of thumb is to make sure it does not exceed 43%. This means that the total of your recurring monthly debt should not exceed 43% of your total monthly gross income.

- **Cost of move (relocation)** - It's going to cost you to move, no matter whether you are moving down the block or to another state. Realistically determine what those costs may be. Will you need to hire movers? Or can you rent a truck on your own? Will you need to store some of your belongings while your house sells? These expenses need to be included in the cost of relocation.

- **Renovation budgets** - Are you going to have to do some repairs on the house you sell in order to get it listed and sold in a reasonable amount of time? Budget for any renovations ahead of time so you'll be prepared.

- **Deposits/costs needed for a new house** - When you enter into a Purchase and Sale Agreement for a new home, you will need an initial earnest money deposit. This does not have to be too much; as a good rule of thumb, plan on 1% - 4% of the purchase price. Additionally, most banks require 20% of the purchase price to come from the Seller's funds for a mortgage. This can be lower depending on the type of mortgage loan, but this is the general rule.

- **Cost of living at new location** - Is your cost of living at your new desired location going to be higher, possibly impacting your standard of living? Be sure to research this, and add this in the equation of your moving costs. By doing so, you will be able to determine whether you'll need to put a nest egg aside so you can continue to meet your standard of living until you are able to either minimize your costs or increase your income.

- **Your current credit score** - If you plan to finance a new house after you sell your current one, the credit score will affect the eligibility and interest rate you get.

UNDERSTAND YOUR MINIMUM TARGET PRICE

Once you understand your future plans, as well as the financial needs to accomplish them, you should develop an understanding of the minimum target price you would want from the sale of your home. Determining your sale price should also take the following into consideration:

- The price needs to cover your current mortgage commitments.
- It can help cover any major bills that you may have, and would like to consider covering as part of this transaction.
- If buying a house after the sale, you will need to have enough funds for the down payment, closing costs, and moving expenses of your future home.
- Take into account any target savings you'd like to obtain through the sale.
- Figure in the commission that will be part of the listing price if you hire a listing agent. The average rate is 5%, but can vary.
- When you close on the house, your closing expenses will also customarily include paying ½ of the real estate transfer tax and preparation of the deed. Transfer taxes are a percentage of the real estate, sale and this percentage differs from state to state.
- Be aware that you will also have to settle on any unpaid taxes due as of the closing date, as well as any bills related to the home that are unpaid up until the closing (utilities, water, cable, etc.).
- If you plan to do any renovations to the home prior to listing it, take the amount of costs for those into consideration.

This target price you determine after figuring all of these variables should be a base price that you would like to obtain from the sale of your home. This will help you determine the feasibility of your decision to sell and relocate. It is not necessary for the current market value of your property to be the same amount you come up with. The goal is for it to be higher. Later on we will discuss what a Comparative Market Analysis (CMA) is (used by real estate agents to determine the current market value of a home), and the importance of a CMA in selling your home. At this stage, determining the minimum target price will help you define your needs, and it will help guide your decision-making process when it comes to selling your home.

SHOULD I SELL, RENT OR STAY?

Once you understand why you want to move, what your financial needs are, and what your target price is, you are on the right path. You can then make better-educated decisions. You will also have a much clearer understanding of your future direction and what to do next.

Depending on your financial situation and/or the market value of the property, you may have to make some tough decisions as to if it is best to sell your property, or possibly, rent it instead. Numerous factors will need to be considered if renting the property is on your list of options. You may have to take into account the varying needs of managing your property remotely. If you plan to rent, you may also need to consider the possibility of having double mortgages.

We could truly write a whole book on just the steps and considerations you will need to take if you are thinking about renting your property. If this is a possibility for you, we would suggest considering the following during your decision-making process:

- Assume your property will be vacant 1-3 months per year
- Assume you will need to budget 30-40 percent of your rental income for maintenance
- Assume your insurance rates will increase by 20% (Plus, you will need to change the type of insurance you have on your property)
- Having two mortgages will affect your ability to borrow
- Having two mortgages, as well as maintenance expenses for two properties, could affect your standard of living

Most of our friends, along with folks we've met over the years, who have made the decision to rent their home as they moved on, ended up taking a big loss due to the struggle in managing the rental property. They ended up selling the property eventually, but by the time they finally were able to, they had become Motivated Sellers because they needed to sell quickly to reduce the monthly outgoing cash flow.

The decision whether to sell, rent, or stay is important to keep in mind, although you can make the final decision a little later on in the process. Your final decision will be based on your minimum price needed to sell the property, coupled with market conditions. It will also take into consideration what it will take to get the property ready.

We truly think the only time you should consider renting the property is if you (a) have enough equity, and (b) you can afford to carry two mortgages for 2-4 months a year. If you have not managed a rental before, our recommendation is that you should only consider whether to stay or sell your house, and remove renting from the list of possibilities.

COUPLES' ACTION SUMMARY

Next-step decisions on future directions is always a family conversation on our side. It is a decision that affects every member of the family; in our experience, it is important to understand your needs and plan it as a team. In our family, we plan our next steps/options as early as possible since we both work long hours, and we have to work as a team to achieve our next steps.

Some of these discussions, especially when it comes to selling your current house and relocating to a new home, may affect work, schools, and/or daily living activities. We like to have some of these discussions over a cup of coffee or over dinner.

1. Discussion on reason for selling, to include other possible options (renting or staying)
2. Discussion on future path and options
3. Discussion on financials
4. Agree on target/range of minimum sales price needed
5. Determine expenses for move
6. Determine future costs of living
7. Making sure credit score(s) falls within requirements needed to obtain a mortgage for the next home (if applicable)
8. Determine ability to carry two homes if property doesn't sell in timeframe needed for move
9. View potential future homes to consider
10. Attend open houses - and take notes of things you like

Working together and dividing the work to allow time to research and plan will go a long way. In the end, remember that you are a team and have similar objectives - a smile, a rose, a dinner, etc. will go a long way to support each other through this process.

NOTES

TASKS

- [ ]
- [ ]
- [ ]
- [ ]
- [ ]
- [ ]
- [ ]
- [ ]
- [ ]

House Selling Process Simplified - Ten Steps

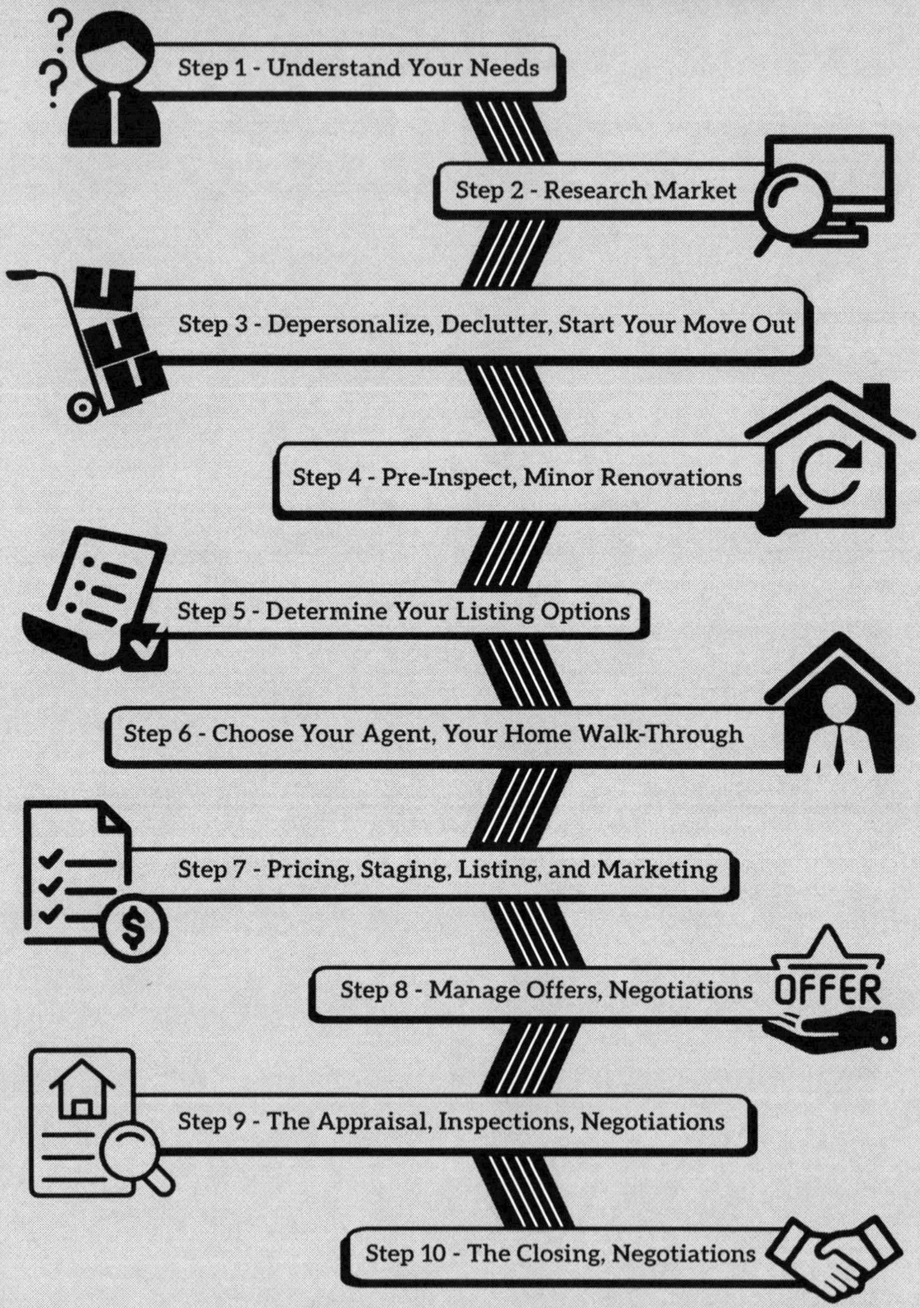

CHAPTER TWO

HOUSE SELLING PROCESS SIMPLIFIED - TEN STEPS

Now that you have decided to sell, understanding the steps and being prepared should speed up and make the process easier.

- Knowledge is power; the steps presented for your consideration in Chapter 1 will help you achieve your financial goals and keep you on track through the selling process.
- Knowing the current market dynamics will help you determine whether your property could be on the market for a longer or shorter period of time. It will help you prepare for negotiating strategies which will be covered later on in this book.
- When you have a CMA (comparative market value) done by a potential listing agent for your property, you will have a better understanding as to whether you should stay put, rent, or sell your property at this given time.
- Knowing your neighborhood and the qualities it offers will prepare you for any questions that may come your way.
- Researching the price range, availability and cost of living for where you would like to relocate will further help you determine whether this is the right move for you. You could be offered a better salary/job at a new location, but if the cost of living and price of homes are too high, will you really be making the right decision?

PREPARATION IS INVALUABLE

The more knowledgeable you are about the process, the more prepared you will be.

We have been involved in the buying and selling of homes across multiple states, CA, NY, VA, MA, MD, MI, PA, FL, and TX, and we have seen that the overall processes and decision-making are essentially the same. The main differences are typically on the contracting side, and engagement with the real-estate agents, as each state has its own set of rules. Regardless of where you reside in the USA, our process and approach will provide the steps and recommendations to help you.

This chapter gives a summary of the detailed steps we discuss throughout the book. Consider this to be the book's Cliff Notes, with the intention of sharing with you a high-level approach and an outline of steps to take, before we dig deeper into the details.

STEP 1 - UNDERSTAND YOUR NEEDS

- Why am I selling? By understanding why you're selling, it will help you in your planning and understanding your timelines.
- What are my future options? Buy understanding where you are moving and what is needed, it will help you in the planning process.
- What is my target budget? With a clear understanding of your budgets and needs, you can make better educated decisions when calculating what is the minimum price that you can accept for your house.
- When do I need to move out by? The process to sell your house right, will take time and effort. By

understanding specific target dates, it will help you organize your overall process timeline.

- Plan and do not rush into it; by planning ahead, the process will go more smoothly and, most probably, you'll be able to get more for your house.

STEP 2 - RESEARCH THE MARKET

- Is it a Buyer's or Seller's Market? We will examine this topic in detail later, but in short the market demand in the area where your house is located will drive the price and, typically, how long your house will be on the market.
- Are there market pricing trends in my neighborhood? Understanding the market trends in your neighborhood may help you determine when you want to list your house.
- What has sold in my neighborhood in the past 6 months? Understanding what has sold in your area and for what price will help you better understand your price points.
- What homes are currently for sale in my neighborhood? This is your competition. Understand how to position your house relative to other properties for sale in your area.
- Document the highlights of your neighborhood. You need to be able to highlight to potential Buyers the features and amenities available in your area, since this will play a part in their decision-making process and help differentiate you from the competition.

STEP 3 - DEPERSONALIZE, DECLUTTER, START YOUR MOVE OUT PREPARATIONS

- You have made the decision to move, so begin your moving process. Starting early will help you in the overall process, making it easier as a whole to plan the sale of your house.
- You want to maximize the space in your house. Packing and moving things out will help the Buyer visualize the space better.
- You want to protect your valuables and personal items.
- You will want to protect your valuables. Plan on packing valuables and personal items away.
- Determine what to keep, donate, sell, or throw away. The process of deciding what to do with the current belongings can be lengthy and difficult.
- Examine local storage options. As part of the process, carefully consider your options and make a decision on where to store your belongings.
- Recruit help from friends, family, and professionals. The process can be overwhelming depending on your house and the items that you have collected over time.

STEP 4 - PRE-INSPECTION / MINOR RENOVATIONS

- Your Buyers will inspect your property as part of the purchase process, and they will, most likely, provide you a list of items to address.
- No home is perfect; ensure you do not have any show-stoppers or items that will require you to rush through the process.

- Pre-inspect the property to develop an understanding of the issues ahead of time, thereby reducing future risk.
- Based on the pre-inspection findings, determine what renovations to address before listing the property.
- By pre-inspecting the property, your minimal investment upfront will establish a baseline of what is needed, better preparing you for negotiations during the agreement process.

STEP 5 - DETERMINE YOUR LISTING OPTIONS

- Are you going to sell the house by owner or leverage a professional real estate agent?
- You can save the commission cost by selling the property by owner, but in order to do so, you should be ready to invest a lot of your personal time and also develop a good understanding of the process, effective marketing, required documentation and real estate laws.
- Selling a house requires a strong understanding of marketing and negotiation skills. We have never had a transaction go through without the need to negotiate.
- Buyers assume that when you're not selling with an agent, you pass the savings on to them; if not priced or shown right, it will affect the whole process.
- The commission is typically split by the Listing and Selling Agents/Agencies (50/50). If you're planning to sell by owner, you may still have to pay the Buyer's Agent if you want agent-based showings. So, keep in mind that by doing it yourself, you may only save yourself 50% of the commission cost.

- Our recommendation is to leverage a professional real estate agent; we believe the commission is always negotiable based on the market.

STEP 6 - CHOOSING YOUR AGENT / YOUR HOME WALK-THROUGH

- Selecting the right real estate agent to list your home will make a big difference in your experience during the sales process; you are hiring a salesperson with experience to represent you.
- You're the hiring manager; plan to interview a number of agents and look to hire the most qualified and experienced one. In the end, you most likely will pay the same commission for an experienced agent or what we refer to as "a junior agent" (one with not as much experience). Do not sell yourself short and succumb to the pressure of hiring the first agent. They are trained salespersons and only make money on commission. They may offer you the world while trying to convince you to list your property with them. Do your homework and check out the facts of their experience and track record.
- It's important to ensure you select an agent with marketing experience and a track record of being a Seller's Agent.
- When selecting an agent, you need to take into account the agency, too. Select an agency that has a successful track record and reputation, as well as an understanding of your neighborhood.
- Once you narrow it down to 1-3 potential agents to represent you, meet individually with each one at your house. Do a walk through during this meeting and

ask the right questions. Afterwards, we recommend you wait at least 24 hours before making your final decision, avoiding the pressure of signing on the spot and allowing yourself time to thoroughly think through who you feel is best to represent you in the sale of your home.

STEP 7 - PRICING, STAGING, LISTING, AND MARKETING

- The Pricing Strategy and the Marketing Strategy are the two key factors that will bring Buyers to your house.
- Curb Appeal and Staging are what will help Buyers determine if the property is appealing to them, and if they can imagine the next phase of their lives in your house.
- It is important to stage your house, either by doing it yourself (DIY), or by leveraging a professional.
- The listing description of your property is as important as your other marketing efforts. The listing description is what Buyers will read first on listing sheets, online, or in newspaper advertisements when searching for potential properties. Like all of us, they may read the first couple of lines and move on. How attentive they are will make more of a difference if you're in a Seller's Market or a Buyer's Market, but regardless of what market you're in, you want to try to capture their interest and maximize your return. The listing description needs to highlight the key points in the first few lines to attract the Buyer right from the get-go. The objective is to hold their interest so they add your house to the short list of homes they decide to look at, rather than pass it by.

- Develop a marketing plan that best highlights and represents your property; use the latest technology, when possible, and leverage the best and most effective marketing approach you can afford.

STEP 8 - MANAGE OFFERS, NEGOTIATIONS

- Depending on how you position your house, the odds are that you will get multiple offers, and you will need to make decisions on which offers to move forward with.
- Key factors include the timing for when you list your property, and when you hold the open house(s) for your property. These factors will impact the probability of getting multiple offers.
- Selecting the right offer will be very important since it is just the start of the negotiation process, and there are a series of steps to follow to successfully get your house sold.
- You need to manage the offers, and qualify them against a number of variables; your professional real estate agent can help you through the process.
- In our experience, it is important to find out more about the Buyers and understand why they wish to buy your house; these variables will play a role in the negotiation process immediately, or later on down the road, in your journey to sell your house.
- Negotiating contract terms with potential Buyers requires you to have a full understanding of each step along the way; your professional real estate agent will help you. Be sure to ask them questions so you have a clear understanding before you sign your name to a Purchase and Sale contract.

- Agreements with potential Buyers on timelines/house closing dates need to be determined upfront.
- Accepting the offer does not mean the deal is done; you still have to go through appraisals, inspections, and the next round of negotiations.

STEP 9 - THE APPRAISAL, INSPECTIONS, NEGOTIATIONS

- Appraisal - Your Buyer or their lender will request a formal appraisal of the property to ensure that the offer price is valid within the market. Challenges with the appraisal may occur if the appraisal value is less than what the Buyer offered. At that stage, you will need to negotiate to determine the next steps forward.
- Inspection - In most cases, the Buyer will request a series of inspections such as home, radon, and termite inspections. No home is perfect, so be prepared. The inspections will usually find issues to report, either minor or major. If you have done your pre-inspection, you should not have any surprises.
- Not all inspectors will find the same issues. Just because you did your pre-inspection, it does not mean that other issues will not show up; that's ok, the list should be shorter and manageable.
- During the inspection process, the Buyer will present you with a list of issues found; the Buyer will usually want to negotiate on how to address the issues. The way you write your contract at the offer stage will determine the options the Buyer has at this point. We always recommend that you write the offer in a way to allow you, as the Seller, to address issues found rather than letting the Buyer walk away.

- Negotiations can be tough, and you have a lot riding on the inspections at this stage. You have invested in getting the house ready, selecting an agent, marketing, showing the property, reviewing offers, and waiting through the inspection timelines; take your time and analyze the pros and cons of different decisions.
- In our experience, it is at this stage in the sales process when most deals fall through. Depending on the market, and the Buyer's requests, you may have to walk away. This should always be an option if planned right.
- After this stage, iIf all goes well with the negotiations, you will need to start planning for moving out and meeting the closing dates.

STEP 10 - THE CLOSING, NEGOTIATIONS

- Once you're through the final negotiation process, you still need to take steps to close on the property.
- Finalizing your move
- The final walk through
- The legal paperwork
- The funds transfer
- Having utilities shut down
- Starting your journey on the next step in your life.

COUPLES' ACTION SUMMARY

Each one of us brings to the table different life experiences, likes, and desires. Working as a team will help leverage the strength of each other. For us, Jinan enjoys the research, going through the details of different properties, and writing; she has an eye for design. On the other hand, CJ likes working in the yard and leading the make-over process, as well as dealing with contractors and real estate agents. One thing that is important to us as a team is to have an understanding of the process and where each would like to play a role, whether individually or together as a team.

1. Having a more concrete plan of your wants and needs which include reasons for moving, financial needs, and timelines
2. Researching the market in your immediate area to determine real estate activity and also possible real estate agents to list your property
3. Setting up a comprehensive plan for decluttering and depersonalizing your home prior to putting it up for sale
4. Pre-inspecting your home and planning minor repairs
5. Reviewing your listing options
6. Researching and interviewing 2-3 listing agents
7. Having a CMA done on your property
8. Discussing each of the stages in the selling process
9. Discussing considerations that could occur during listing and selling the property

We truly believe that you need to be informed and have an understanding of the process in order to maximize your return on your investment and reduce the stress levels that are involved in this process. Take your time to review all of the available options and plan them out early and ahead of time.

NOTES

TASKS

Develop an Understanding of Market; Buyer's vs. Seller's Markets

The value of your house will be driven by market demand. The more people that are looking to buy in your neighborhood, the better value you'll get for your home.

Understand what different negotiating skills will be required when an offer is made in a Buyer's Market vs. a Seller's Market.

The real estate market is always changing. It is dynamic and affected by a wide range of factors.

Supply and demand for a given area drive the market price.

Different geographical areas will have varying factors affecting price; look closely at your location when making the analysis.

Buyers will have more options in a Buyer's Market and can have better negotiation power over Sellers due to the large number of houses for sale in a given area.

Buyers will have fewer options in a Seller's Market and will have less negotiation power over a Seller due to the limited number of houses for sale in a given area.

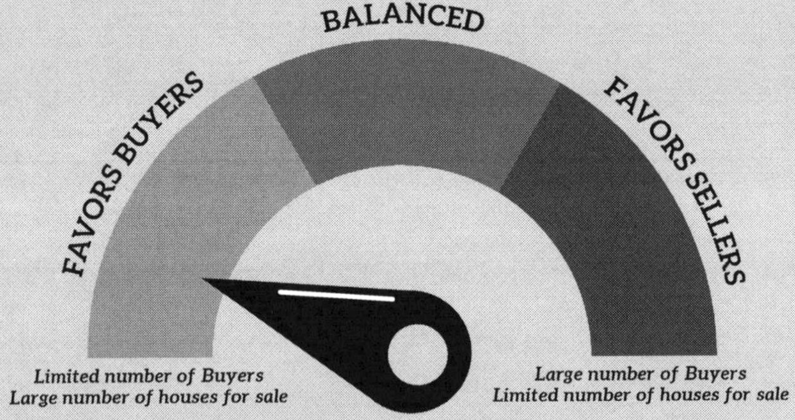

BUYERS MARKET

Large number of houses on the market

Buyers have a lot of options, can offer less for property

Buyers have more negotiation power

Houses tend to stay longer on market

SELLERS MARKET

Limited number of houses on the market

Buyers willing to compete and offer higher prices for property

Sellers have more negotiation power

Houses sell faster

CHAPTER THREE

DEVELOP AN UNDERSTANDING OF MARKET; BUYER'S VS. SELLER'S MARKET

The value of your house will be driven by market demand. The more people that are looking to buy in your neighborhood, the better value you'll get for your home.

- Understand what different negotiating skills will be required when an offer is made in a Buyer's market vs. a Seller's Market
- The real estate market is always changing. It is dynamic and affected by a wide range of factors
- Supply and demand for a given area will drive the market price
- Different geographical areas will have different demands; look at your location when making the analysis
- Buyers will have more options in a Buyer's Market and can have better negotiation power over Sellers due to the large number of houses for sale in a given area.
- Buyers will have fewer options in a Seller's Market and will have less negotiation power over Seller due to the limited number of houses for sale in a given area.

UNDERSTAND THE MARKET

It is important to know the current market in order to know your selling process..

WHY DOES IT MATTER TO ME?

There are a lot of different factors that determine how fast a home sells. The value and demand for your house will change depending on the number of Buyers looking to buy your home. The more Buyers competing for your property, the more likely you are to sell your property faster and get the highest value for it. The Seller's Market vs. Buyer's Market difference is based on the market competition. How much competition you have will determine:

- How many people will be looking at houses in your area
- The selling price of your property
- The potential number of offers you will have on your property
- Your negotiation power over potential offers
- The total number of available properties in your area

The Buyer's Market vs. Seller's Market is a factor you should be aware of as part of the property selling process, but it's not a guarantee that your property will sell quickly or remain on the market for a long time. Regardless of the market conditions, we suggest you become knowledgeable and prepared for the current market conditions. Do your best to position your property right, and take the market into consideration as part of your planning.

WHAT IS A BUYER'S MARKET?

In a Buyer's Market, the "For Sale" signs on properties are there for a long time, maybe months. That's because there are more Sellers looking to sell homes than there are Buyers looking to buy them. Buyers typically have a lot of options in this type of market, and they can try to negotiate on reducing the price or asking for more concessions on repairs and/or Seller's coverage of the Buyer's portion of closing costs. As a Seller, you have to decide if you are willing to negotiate on the price and/or determine how to best differentiate and/or negotiate to get your property sold. At times, if you are not getting what you think the market needs to offer, you may have to consider removing your house from the market and waiting until the market changes.

Some indicators of a Buyer's Market include:

- A lot of houses are for sale in your neighborhood and surrounding areas
- Homes are on the market for a longer period of time
- People are lowering the prices of their home in order to move the property and be more competitive

WHAT IS A SELLER'S MARKET?

In the neighborhood, in a Seller's Market, the "For Sale" signs don't stay up long and you see a lot of "pending" or "sold" signs on properties. That's because there are more Buyers looking for homes than there are homes for sale in the market. This creates additional competition for each home, and gives Sellers more negotiating power in terms of price and concessions on repairs and closing costs.

Some indicators of a Seller's Market include:

- Fewer homes, if any, are for sale in your neighborhood and surrounding areas
- Homes are on the market for a short time and go under agreement quickly. Sometimes they are under contract on the very same day they are listed
- People are looking to sell at asking price or higher, and many times there are multiple offers made on a property, including offers exceeding the listing price of the property.
- Sellers are less apt to negotiate and will be in a position to insist on an offer without any additional contingencies.

DO SELLER'S AND BUYER'S MARKETS CHANGE OVER TIME?

One important thing to note about the property market is that it's always in a state of change. Sometimes the market is favorable to Buyers, and sometimes it's favorable to Sellers. Understanding the type of market you are currently in, and market timing, are imperative in making decisions that will help you be best prepared.

One of the core drivers that affect the markets, even in hot markets, is what drives people to move in and out of a given neighborhood. For example, a lot of people do not move during the school year due to the fact that they do not want to pull their kids from a school in the middle of the school year. Therefore, demand for housing in the summer season may be higher than during other seasons and this can affect how many people will be looking at a given property. In our own investments and personal properties, we have had more success in buying properties during the winter season, and listing properties in March/April, prior to the summer season.

In addition to supply and demand due to seasonal effects of folks moving/leaving the area, other factors have an effect on the demand for housing in a given area. Those factors are typically driven by economic situations. Some examples include:

- A major business leaving an area, creating unemployment for their workers and fewer employment opportunities
- A major business moving into an area presenting new job opportunities, along with possible relocations of workers to the area
- The area becoming a hot spot due to local economic investments and business growth, new highways, proximity to hospitals and municipalities, etc.
- General demographics of area
- The growth of an area due to improvements in security and/or crime reduction
- The decline of the area due to criminal activity and drug problems
- Great school system causing many young families desiring to move into the area

PLANNING AN APPROACH FOR YOUR HOME, REGARDLESS OF MARKET

We have learned the hard way that understanding market timing, coupled with a well-thought out approach, can maximize your return and save you a lot of heartburn and headaches. Even if it is a Buyer's Market, getting your property ready, coupled with the right marketing and real estate agent, will make a tremendous difference.

Depending on the market, your approach will vary in regards to pricing, staging, and negotiations—especially during the planning stage. As you read through this book, we will provide different recommendations for each stage based on whether you're in a Seller's Market or a Buyer's Market. Regardless of the market type, however, the Seller's steps to maximize your return on investment will be the same.

CONSIDERATIONS IN A BUYER'S MARKET

There are several considerations when planning to list your house in a Buyer's Market. One important thing to realize is that in this market where there are numerous homes for sale, the Buyers have more options. Don't feel defeated by the large inventory of homes. Remember, all you need is one Buyer to purchase your house.

- You may not have multiple offers. If you do receive a qualified offer, you need to take the extra time and effort to work through the issues.
- You need to be aware that you will have a lot of competition on the market, and therefore get your house in the best shape possible. Decluttering and minor renovations will be more important in a Buyer's Market. We also recommend that you do a pre-inspection of the property. We believe in pre-inspection whenever selling a property, but we highly recommend it in a Buyer's Market.
- Hiring the right real estate agent and marketing the property effectively are always key factors, but especially in a Buyer's Market. Unless you are great at staging,

getting professional help to best showcase your house is extremely important because Buyers will have several home options—yours will need to stand out among the crowd!

Major factors in successfully selling your home, particularly in a Buyer's Market, include getting professional help to best prepare your house to show and hiring the right real estate agent who is experienced in selling in a Buyer's Market.

CONSIDERATIONS IN A SELLER'S MARKET

There are several things to consider when planning to list your house in a Seller's Market. You will want to maximize the value of your house by getting your house show-ready, and strategically planning your marketing ahead of time to generate multiple offers, even though you only need one. It's important to choose the right offer and best position your property to maximize your return.

- Marketing will be key to maximize the return on your house; you want to push your property to create a competitive bidding scenario, and you want to increase the demand for your property.
- Having your house ready to show its best will still be very important; going through our recommendation of decluttering and minor renovations will help maximize your return.

COUPLES' ACTION SUMMARY

Regardless as to whether you are in a Seller's Market or a Buyer's Market, we believe that through following a systematic process and approach, you should be able to sell your house. The tough questions in a Buyer's Market will be at what price to sell and what is needed to be competitive in the market. This goes back to your needs and timing desires for selling your home. The real estate market truly fluctuates, and people are always in the process of moving in or moving out of a given area. In order for you to make educated decisions as a team, together, you need to understand what is going on with the housing market at your current location, as well as the location/neighborhood you plan to move to after selling your home. Both will affect decisions on how to proceed.

1. Determine market conditions (Buyer's Market vs Seller's Market)
2. Determine who you will choose to be your real estate agent (strongly recommended)
3. Finalize marketing plan based on market conditions
4. Go over any additional considerations based on market conditions
5. Recommended pre-inspection
6. Plan to get your home ready to show prior to putting on the market, include professional help if needed, in order to showcase your house in the best way possible

By understanding the various market conditions, you can truly set expectations upfront. Realize that you need to make decisions and maybe sacrifices in order to move the deal forward. In the end, selling a home is a huge financial transaction that will affect your bottom line. As a team, it will be important to continue to have discussions about market conditions as you plan to maximize the return on your investment.

NOTES

NOTES

TASKS

- [ ]
- [ ]
- [ ]
- [ ]
- [ ]
- [ ]
- [ ]
- [ ]
- [ ]

Your House, Your Neighborhood

People tend to look for a real estate agent who is familiar with their neighborhood to help them sell.

Think how you would describe your neighborhood if you were the salesperson.

Identify the cool things and/or resources that you think important to highlight.

Research your area in more depth to highlight different features and resources.

How far is it to the hospital? Police Station? School? Grocery Store?
Does the bus stop at or close by the house?

Are there places to go to get involved in the community?

Is there a neighborhood watch in the area?

What makes the neighborhood stand out for you?

Drive all the different routes that lead to your home.
Which one is the most appealing?

Distance to a major highway is also an important for many.

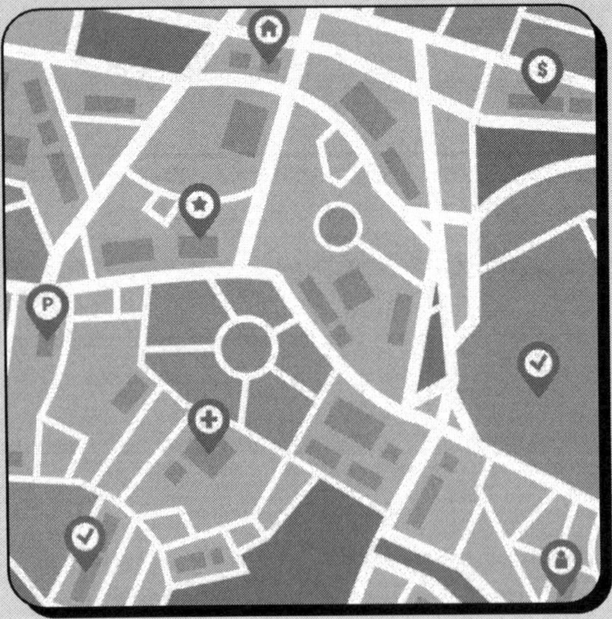

Cool Things About Your Neighborhood

- *Schools*
- *Restaurants*
- *Retail Areas*
- *Walkability*
- *Access to Public Transportation*
- *Farmers Markets*
- *Parks/Playgrounds*
- *Community Clubs and Pools*
- *Etc.*

CHAPTER FOUR

YOUR HOUSE, YOUR NEIGHBORHOOD

A lot of people look for a real estate agent who is familiar with their neighborhood in order to effectively market and sell their property, but we truly believe you know your neighborhood best.

- Think how you would describe your neighborhood if you were the salesperson
- Identify the cool things and/or resources that you would like to highlight
- Different potential Buyers will have different interests. Research your area in more depth to highlight different interests and resources that you may not have originally thought of
- How far is it to the hospital? Police Station? School? Grocery Store? Does the bus stop near the house, or do children need to be driven to school?
- Are there places to go to get involved in the community?
- Is there a neighborhood watch? Do neighbors look out for the safety of each other and keep each other informed of what's happening in the area?
- What is it that really makes the neighborhood stand out for you? Express it to your potential Buyers. Your excitement will get them excited.

- Drive all the different routes that lead to your home. Which one is the most appealing? Make sure the listing agent is aware of what would be the most desirable route to take the Buyer.
- Know what the best route is for a Buyer to commute to work. Distance to a major highway is important for many.

KNOW YOUR NEIGHBORHOOD

Gathering specific information about your neighborhood and sharing this with Buyers is a great marketing tool.

YOU UNDERSTAND YOUR NEIGHBORHOOD BEST

When Buyers are looking for a house, they look in a specific neighborhood for a certain reason; a lot of times they may be looking at different areas and may not be very informed about all the different offerings that make your neighborhood more attractive. For us, we have started building a neighborhood binder that we have available for Sellers to see with highlights. Consider this as an additional tool in your marketing tool chest. We have seen it used and we have used it in the sale of our own properties. We believe it adds value to your house, and it does not take much to put together. You can even make it a fun family project.

DEVELOPING A NEIGHBORHOOD BINDER

If you have ever traveled and stayed at hotels, one of the items you'll often see is a binder of all the things you can do locally. In fact, most hotels on our road trips also have a special display of pamphlets that highlight all the things you can do in the area. You need to think of your neighborhood in a similar manner. Based on our own property searches, when Buyers are looking to buy a new home, they have an idea about where they want to be in a general sense, but their search may span multiple neighborhoods. As an example, if they are looking for specific school ratings or a place within a specific travel distance from work/school, they will consider multiple neighborhoods, examining the pros and cons of the different neighborhoods/houses as they narrow down their options as part of the selection process. Finding a new place to live is a stressful process to the Buyers and they will need to consider what's around their new neighborhood. This is your opportunity to communicate and highlight things you would like them to know about their potential new community. Below are sections or information that you may consider including in the binder.

- **The Welcome Letter** - We always start by saying "Welcome!" and providing a brief history, as well as a summary of the area with an explanation as to why we have put together this binder for them.
- **House History** - If you have completed any major renovations, and/or if you would like to showcase some before and after pictures of improvements you've made, this can help Buyers appreciate the work and investment that went into the property
- **Neighborhood History/Future** - Include any information about the past that the Buyer would be interested in and also include whether there are future community plans that will increase the value of the property. For example, add information of any major industry/factory/company relocating to the area, as well as other plans that could increase the value of the property.

- **Schools/Universities** - Even if you don't have kids, it's good to mention the schools pyramid, particularly if you're in a highly rated school district. In addition if you're within 20-30 minutes of a major university, it is worth mentioning. If you're not in a highly rated school district, see if you can find anything special about the school district that can be mentioned. In general, good school districts can have a major impact on real estate values.

- **Public Transportation** - If your house is close to a transit station and/or has other public transportation within walking distance, the Buyer will be interested. For example, one of the reasons we bought our current property is due to the fact it was in walking distance to public transportation to the city. Both traffic and parking are issues in the city, and by having public transportation available, we can be in the city in 20 minutes. since public transportation has special routes around traffic.

- **Walking/Parks** - Is the neighborhood walkable? Does it have nice sidewalks? Do you have trails and parks? Do a lot of folks regularly walk, run, and/or take their dogs for a walk in the neighborhood and/or park? Are there street lamps so the neighborhood is well-lit in the evenings? If yes to any of these questions, you should highlight them.

- **Local Activities** - Highlight farmers markets, community centers, pools, theaters, other local attractions and activities—these are places where you can not only get out of the house, but are great places to make neighborhood friends.

- **Community Events** - Does your community hold any special events? Our local community holds and hosts a wide range of events throughout the year around the community pool. It was a pleasant surprise for us to find out about it and would have definitely added to our decision to buy into the neighborhood.
- **Community Watch** - Does the community have a local community watch group and/or community communications, news and updates? Do they use apps such as Nextdoor to keep the community informed? Is there a Home Owner Association? Be sure to mention these since safety will be very important to Buyers.
- **Shopping Centers/Retail Access** - Many Buyers want quick access to retail and delivery services. If you have local shopping centers and/or malls etc., you should list some.
- **Fire Departments, Hospitals, Urgent Care** - Being close enough to get to a hospital or doctor's office quickly is key for many people. List names/distance of some of the local services.
- **Sports/Exercise** - A lot of Buyers want access to sports centers and/or to a local gym. If your property is close and/or within minutes of a gym/sports complex, it may be beneficial to list.
- **Restaurants/Entertainment** - Having great restaurants, shopping, and markets are an added value. If some are nearby, list at least a few different ones. Also, list the nearby town center or downtown area, movie theaters, other theaters, bars, and nightlife. Note if your neighborhood has hot spots within walking distance or a short ride away. Today many Buyers prefer Uber/Lyft rather than driving.

- **Delivery Services** - Today, more and more home Buyers rely on delivery services for food, groceries and laundry services. If your area has those available, you should list them.

Take your time and build it as you go. We will come back to the neighborhood binder in the marketing section, but for now, we recommend you start capturing notes, brochures, menus, etc., and organizing the information needed.

COUPLES' ACTION SUMMARY

We have learned that we need to put ourselves in other people's shoes in order for us to make the right decisions. Whether we are getting a property ready for a rental, or a property ready for sale, we have to always consider what people are looking for, and what little things will make a difference in the decision making process for folks to move into a given house. We have come to the realization that the neighborhood is more important than the house itself for most families when it comes to buying a house. If they can afford the neighborhood, they will look at that as their first option. If they cannot afford the neighborhood, they will start looking at secondary options based on the priorities of their family's needs .

That being said, look back and see why you moved into your area and consider how to help showcase it in particular ways to best appeal to Buyers.

1. Research neighborhood in more depth; know resources, routes, highlights, schools, activities, etc.
2. Collect brochures, local newspaper, coupons, menus, etc. that may be of interest to Buyers
3. Create a detailed binder to include Welcome letter, history of home, resources, restaurants, attractions, etc.

We recommend that you do this exercise early on and talk about it as a couple/family. It is interesting that the things we have found out about some of our neighborhoods/communities that we have lived in and/or owned properties in, we would have loved to have known about earlier. If you find interesting, new and fun things in your area, such as great restaurants and/or activities, why not plan an outing and discover? Use the excuse of research to better discover your current area and have fun doing it!

NOTES

TASKS

- [ ]
- [ ]
- [ ]
- [ ]
- [ ]
- [ ]
- [ ]
- [ ]
- [ ]

Depersonalize and Declutter

Naturally, Buyers are seeking a home that they would want to live in. Your goal is to help your Buyers visualize a home that is their own.

You have a personal attachment to your home; realize selling is a hard step.

Curb appeal and first impressions make a great difference.

Taking basic steps now can help sell your house faster and receive better offers.

Planning now in support of your move can ease stress for you and the Buyers.

Create the space and home that your Buyers would love to call home.

Showing every room decluttered of extras will add appeal and value to your house.

Don't forget to safeguard your valuables and precious memories.

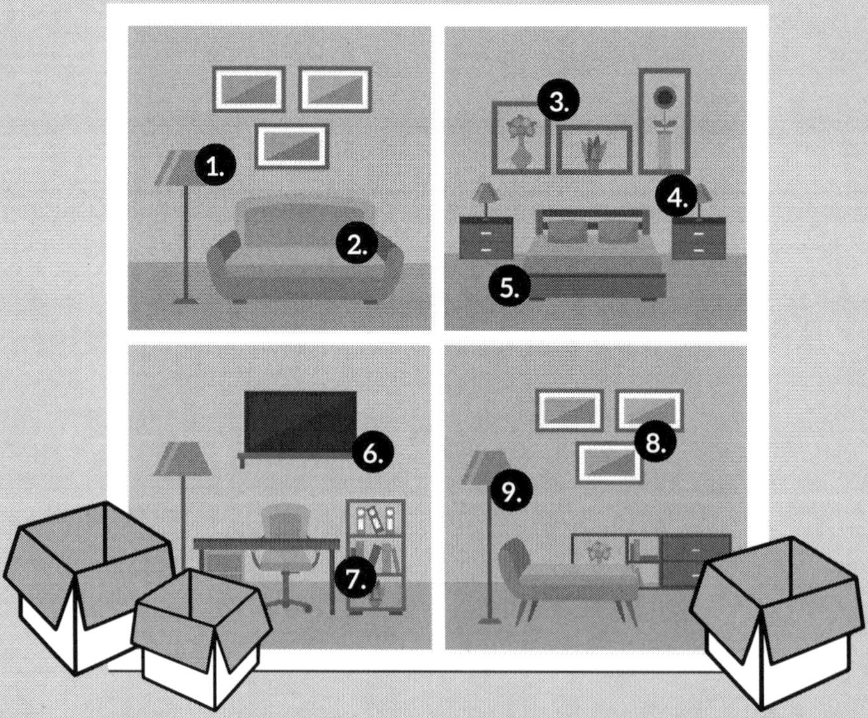

CHAPTER FIVE

DEPERSONALIZE AND DECLUTTER

Buyers are looking for a home that they want to live in. You want to help your Buyers visualize a home that is theirs—a home that is cared for, organized, and has lots of space to meet their needs.

- You have a personal attachment to your home; realize this will be a hard step
- Curb appeal and first impressions make a big difference
- Taking basic steps can help sell your house faster and with the potential to receive a higher offer
- Planning and accomplishing some of these tasks now in support of your move can ease stress for both you and the Buyers
- Create the space and home that your Buyers want to call home
- Showing every room decluttered of extras will add more appeal and value to your house
- Safeguard your valuables and precious memories by getting them ready to move with you
- Think of this as the first step in your move and start your packing early on in the planning process

THE HOUSE LOOKS BETTER

"It is amazing how good the house looks when decluttered; it looks much better than when we lived in it!" This is your objective for the decluttering process. You may fall in love with the house again, and it will make it harder for you to let go, but that is your goal—you want the Buyers to fall in love with it too!

TRANSFORMING YOUR HOME TO YOUR HOUSE TO SELL

From our own experience, and from helping family and friends sell their homes—especially after they have lived in them for years—we know first-hand that this is one of the hardest steps in selling your home.

Most of us have spent years in our homes. We have personalized them and made them our own. Throughout the house, we add pictures, knick-knacks, much-loved furniture, and assorted collections that hold strong memories. Now you have made the decision to move on. It is important that you consider transforming your home to the house you're selling that Buyers will find most appealing. And don't forget that wherever you move to, your new living quarters/house will soon feel like home, containing all these personal belongings.

If you consider that you are just relocating with a process of cleaning out unwanted or seldom-used items, this will help as a start. We truly believe this step of depersonalizing and decluttering has added value to you as a Seller too. It will help you get your personal items packed away, knowing they are with you to move on; they are not part of the house you're leaving behind. Through this transformation process of packing what you want to bring, and donating and throwing away any unwanted items, the place you're living in now will become less your home. This will make it easier on you emotionally. It will transform to the house and/or product you're selling which will help you move on in your life as you look forward to your future direction. Importantly, it will also help you market your property in the best possible way.

WILL IT MAKE A DIFFERENCE?

Most Buyers are looking for a place to call home. We truly believe simple steps from depersonalizing to decluttering will make all the difference in how fast you can sell your house and will also make a difference in the offer price.

People who are buying a house to live in and call home are very different from those purchasing a home as an investment. A Buyer who falls in love with your house because it meets their needs will typically move quickly and is willing to offer a higher price (if they can get the right financing) to buy your house.

By packing your personalized items and decluttering your house, you are allowing the Buyer to see the space and imagine themselves living in it. You are allowing your Buyers to get emotionally attached to their future home by helping them best visualize living in the property you are selling.

IMPORTANCE OF PLANNING

Be willing to make the tough decisions on whether you should keep or give/throw away your belongings. We are always surprised with the amount of material (stuff) we have accumulated over the years. The fact that you're assessing your house, objectively and thoroughly, from the outside in, can, and most likely will, seem like a Herculean task. At times, it is, but do not become overwhelmed. With the right approach and planning, this can become an easier and less stressful process. Some of the steps that can help make this process easier include:

- **Planning your move early** - A lot of Sellers wait to start planning their move only after they list their property, or even when they get an offer. By doing so, they add a lot of undue pressure on themselves. Once you decide to put your house up for sale, our recommendation is that you mentally start thinking and planning your move out of the house. This will help immensely.
- **Planning your storage** - We have learned over the years that it is important to highlight every room in the house. Early on when we sold our first house, we used one of the bedrooms and the garage to store our personal items. Today, we strongly recommend renting a storage unit in a nearby storage facility. Most storage facilities offer the first month for free, and the monthly rate is low. In addition, some offer free use of a moving truck. By placing most of your personal items in storage, you will allow the Buyers to envision how they'll arrange their furniture best throughout the house to fit their needs. In that way, they can begin to envision your house as their own.
- **Plan your approach** - It is always a hard decision on what to do with your personal items, your furniture, and all the knick-knacks and other items you have accumulated over the years. Our recommendation is to look at the content of your house and group them into multiple categories such as:
    - **Keep** – These are the items you've decided to keep, either for necessity or for personal reasons.
    - **Donate/Sell** – These are items you no longer want or need. You can put them in a yard sale, or you can sell through an online board. What doesn't sell, you can always donate.

- **Throw away** – This group consists of items that are just ready to be tossed. No one would want them, and you don't need them.
- **Incentive as part of the sale** – These are items that look good in the house to stage for photos and showings of the house, but you do not want to keep them. However, they may be of interest to the Buyer, also, and could become part of the purchase.
- **Undecided** – If undecided, we would keep these items in one pile, and you will later make a decision to keep, store, or dispose of them. It is okay to be undecided about some items.
- **Would like to replace** – These items have value, and are necessary to hold onto while you are selling the house, but you do not really want to keep when you move. However, you need them until you do move. Try to keep these to a minimum and as soon as you no longer need them, put them in the throw away or give away pile. These also, however, could be of interest to the Buyers and part of the sale of the house.

Once you are ready to categorize your items, you are one step closer to starting the process.

- **Plan your help** - It is a major effort to unclutter. We recommend that you develop a list of people who can help you. The list can include friends, family, neighbors, and even hired help. A co-worker of mine threw a big barbeque event for friends and family to come and help in the process. Great idea!
- **Plan your moving materials list** - It is a major effort to move, so we recommend you start getting your boxes and packing materials early on. You may be surprised

by the cost of the moving boxes when compared to the amount of belongings that you have to pack, particularly for boxes you will typically use once. We have leveraged a number of online sites with folks selling their moving boxes and materials for cheap. In addition, we typically keep the shipping boxes for any online orders because these are nice moving boxes; they are easy to fold and do not take a lot of space in the garage. They have come in handy over time, even when we are not moving. If you work in an office that orders paper for the copier(s), the boxes that a case of paper comes in make great moving boxes. Place a couple of boxes in each room and just fill, seal, and label each box as time permits.

- **Plan your rooms, one room at a time** - As part of your planning, we recommend you go through all the rooms and outside areas and make a list for each room/area as to what needs to be packed, thrown away, given away, etc.
- **Establish a schedule with target dates** - It will be hard to establish dates at this time of the planning process, but once you have the boxes set up in all areas and rooms, you can set the duration you want for packing and decluttering each given area/room [i.e basement (4 days), guest bedroom (3 days), etc.] This will help keep you on track regarding time needed for packing and preparing. Depending on your schedule and the amount of clutter that you have, it may take a few days, a few weeks, or a couple of months to complete this process.
- **Start now, take baby steps as part of your daily routines** - You have already set a plan for each area of your house, as well as high-level dates that you would

like to achieve. Be flexible, however, without losing sight of your major plan. Life events may change your timeline. As long as you work toward the dates, one day at a time, and you work on it as a team and with a plan, you will accomplish this task with the least amount of stress.

DEPERSONALIZE

Your personal items and your life are yours; you want to keep your family and personal items yours. When you plan to sell your house, your memories and personal items should be ready to move with you. This will also help the new Buyer visualize their own items in their new future home. You truly want the Buyer to focus on the potential of the property they are looking at. It's important for them to envision living comfortably in your house with memories of their own. It is good to eliminate as many distractions from them being able to do this. Therefore, if you don't need to have your personal items easily accessible, pack them up as soon as you can.

It is also important to note that you will have a large number of people going through your house when no one else is around. Most, if not all, will be strangers. We have had some of our personal items "walk away." If you have a collection of baseball cards or other valuable items, for example, you should keep them safe and stored away before allowing any showings of your home, even if the listing agent will be present and watching. Again, it's very important to pack up personal items prior to showing the property. This can include family photos, trophies, awards, collectables, specialized décor, and any other items that hold special meaning to you. Personal documentation should always be stored and locked away to prevent anyone from obtaining confidential information and engaging in identity theft. Computers and other electronic devices should be removed or locked so no information is accessible. Do you have an Alexa or Google Home device? Remove or disable it. It would be nice to believe everyone is loyal and honest, but, as most of us have come to know, that's just not the case. Better to be safe than sorry.

With our suggested approach to decluttering and depersonalizing at an early stage for your move, you'll be helping yourself, as well as the Buyer. You'll also be staying safe.

DECLUTTER

Now that you have identified your personal items, it is time to look at the next steps. When categorizing the rest of the items, our recommendation is that if you have not used an item in the past two or three years, consider donating, selling at a garage sale, or throwing out. The more you declutter, the cleaner and more spacious your house will appear to prospective Buyers. Here are a few easy steps to get you started:

- **Check your curb appeal** - First impressions are important and will set the tone for the walk-through of your property. Make sure your yard is clear of any debris and unnecessary items have been removed. Consider pressure-washing driveways and walkways, as well as other areas needed like garage doors, gutters, siding, etc.
- **Start with the least used rooms** - Take care of all spaces; potential Buyers will open all closets and go through every room.
- **Walk through the house** - See how you can maximize the living areas by moving furniture out. You want the space to look as big as possible, uncluttered and inviting.

- **Hallways** - Make sure the hallways are clear and open. Too many items on the walls can also make a hallway look narrower and closed in. Minimize.
- **Living room** - Many of us have a lot of items in the living room. Reduce the amount so the space seems bigger.
- **Kitchen** - This is an area that Buyers will pay particularly close attention to. Make sure you reduce the amount of cooking ware, unclutter drawers and cabinets, and make sure your countertops stay clean and clear. Also make sure your extra appliances are stored neatly in cabinets, closets, or the utility room.
- **Bathrooms** - Yet another area Buyers will examine closely. Visualizing brooms, vacuum cleaners, mops, etc., neatly stored represents structure and good storage space. Organize essentials in a neat and pleasant way within cabinets and/or on an uncluttered shelf.
- **Bedrooms** - The family structure of your Buyers may be different than your family structure. What may have been a bedroom for you could be a home office for them, or vice-versa. Minimize your furnishings and stage your bedroom in the most attractive way, with plenty of open, empty space. Make sure tops of bureaus and tabletops are dusted and cleared of any unnecessary items. Keep wall hangings/pictures to a minimum. Help the Buyer visualize putting a nice television on the wall, or being able to fit their king sized bed in the master bedroom.

COUPLES' ACTION SUMMARY

We would say that the process of decluttering is a process coupled with high stress and emotional attachments to items. At least that is the case for us and almost every one that we know that had to go through the process of selling their home, which is quite different from the process of selling an investment property. Your house has been the place where you have worked hard and created cherished memories over time. It has value and now you have to make a decision whether to keep or let go of it. The moment you decide to move, you also need to begin making decisions on what you will take with you as a couple or family. You will need to discuss this fact and work it together.

1. Plan your move
2. Plan where you will store furniture, personal items, etc. until the move
3. Get boxes for moving
4. Go through each room—depersonalize and declutter; remember to also do this with closets, cabinets and drawers. Plan who will be helping you move

One thing that has worked well for us as a couple is that we do our walk throughs with a checklist for each room, and we discuss what we want to keep/let go of prior to even starting the process of packing/moving stuff or even deciding on storage options. By going through this process, you'll be able to better understand what boxes are needed for different rooms. There are boxes that will work best for dresses and suits, while others will be best for dishes and breakables, etc. Additionally, if you had travel suitcases, you may want to use those for packing clothes, etc.

The one piece of advice that we can offer through this process is to try and make it fun while making it part of your daily routine for a while.

NOTES

NOTES

TASKS

- [ ]
- [ ]
- [ ]
- [ ]
- [ ]
- [ ]
- [ ]
- [ ]
- [ ]
- [ ]

Pre-Inspection and Minor Renovations

Knowledge is power; avoid surprises.

By planning ahead you can achieve the following:

- *You will be better prepared to address any challenges later on.*
- *You can avoid last-minute surprises.*
- *You will have more control over the closing process and ultimately be in a better position to negotiate.*
- *You can avoid the stress that is typically part of the inspection process.*
- *Taking care of renovations noted during the home inspection will help sell your home faster.*

REDUCE RISK:

✔ Be Prepared
✔ Be Proactive
✔ Be Smart

SELL YOUR HOME FASTER BY INVESTING IN A PRE-INSPECTION

CHAPTER SIX

PRE-INSPECTION AND MINOR RENOVATIONS

Knowledge is power; you will avoid surprises and have time to plan and address issues early on by being proactive.

- A pre-inspection can help you address any Buyer inspection challenges later on
- You can avoid last minute surprises by knowing issues ahead of time
- You can get offers faster if you're willing to disclose the inspection on which issues are already addressed
- You will have more control over the closing process and be in a better position to negotiate
- You can avoid typical stress that is part of the inspection process
- Taking care of renovations noted on a home inspection will help sell your house faster
- Investment is minimal upfront with great return later on

PRE-INSPECTION PREPARES YOU FOR THE UNEXPECTED

Be proactive, rather than reactive. This will be beneficial to both you, as the Seller, and to the Buyer.

SHOULD I HAVE AN INSPECTION BEFORE LISTING MY PROPERTY

Our experience has shown over the years that one of the toughest phases of getting the house sold, after an offer has been accepted, is the inspection process. The inspection process is very stressful for both Seller and Buyer. A Buyer may walk away due to finding an issue, or demand a lot of renegotiations because of issues discovered during the inspection. They may use this discovery as a way to reduce their offer significantly. You, as the Seller, may find you are left without a Buyer on your house and much time has been wasted. You may also discover that a major expense is needed to get it back on the market.

One of the main reasons to do a pre-inspection is to know ahead of time what issues/necessary repairs may exist that the Buyer may find during their own inspection prior to purchasing your home. It's wise to avoid surprises, and also important to note that the Buyers, most likely, are going to request a home inspection to be done as part of the process. By having a pre-inspection, you are ahead of the game and know what you may be facing. Also, repairs needed on a home can reduce an appraisal that follows, and an appraisal is required for any bank financing.

One of our friends needed to list a house to settle an estate. They were unaware of the condition and age of the roof, furnace, etc. The inspection was done prior to listing, and it was shared with potential Buyers. This proved to be very helpful information and aided in generating a quick sale. Although the Buyer also needed a home inspection done by the bank providing the financing, it was well worth the investment by the Seller and proved to be a wise decision.

If you have lived in your house for a short period of time and/or you still have an old inspection, you may want to revisit that inspection report. In our experience, regardless of how long you've lived in your house or how old it is, there could be issues you're unaware of that can affect the sale of your house.

Doing a pre-inspection does have a cost associated with it. We feel it is a good investment for selling your house quickly and with the least amount of complications that may arise during the process of doing so.

ADVANTAGES OF PRE-INSPECTION

- **Reduce your risks and negotiation due to inspection** - Every sale that we have done, we have had to negotiate after the house inspection. At times, we ended up with a long list of issues that needed to be fixed, and we have even had to put a house we owned and had under agreement, back on the market due to inspection findings.
- **Avoid the cancelled contract woes** - If the Buyer decides to cancel the contract due to the findings of the inspection report, a canceled contract will show up on your home's property history on the MLS. You will have to answer questions from future Buyers as to why the offer fell through. This could affect how quickly the next Buyer may commit to moving forward with an offer on your property.
- **Understand the condition of your house** - By having a pre-inspection done prior to listing your home, you can find any issues with your property early on, giving you the time to address the ones you believe will hinder the sale of your property.
- **Avoid the rush factor** - When an inspection identifies issues after an offer has been accepted, fixing the issues will have to be done under specific time constraints. If

you do not have a contractor lined up to do the repairs, you may end up paying a lot more for the repairs in order to meet tight deadlines.

- **Support the Pricing Strategy** - You need to price your house based on the house condition; the inspection will help you better define the issues you want to fix to support the target listing price.
- **Win Confidence** - A good inspection report can win confidence and trust with the Buyer, avoid any pitfalls that may arise during the pre-closing process, and speed the sale of your home.

DISADVANTAGES OF PRE-INSPECTION

- **Understanding Disclosure Laws** - Different states have different disclosure laws. In certain states, you may be legally required to disclose all the major issues the pre-inspection uncovers to the Buyer. You will need to understand the disclosure laws of your state. For us it is not an issue, since we believe in karma; if we know of an issue, we either have to fix it, or take it into account on our sale price of the house.
- **Budget Challenges** - Once you know about the issues, you need to figure out how to address them; budget upfront what needs to be fixed or be willing to negotiate a finding as part of the sale process.
- **Slowing down the sales process** - The issues you find through the pre-listing inspection may make it more difficult to sell your house within your original desired timeline. You will need to make decisions based on findings, but knowing about the issues now, is much better than finding about it after the offer has been accepted.

- **Additional Cost** - You will have to pay to have this inspection done by a certified inspector, which is relatively minor compared to the bigger picture of selling your house.

MINOR RENOVATIONS/REPAIRS

The inspection report will provide a punch list for you to address identified issues with the property. It will also prepare you for necessary repairs needing to be done and/or disclosed. Over the years, we have come to the conclusion that painting, minor renovations, and needed repairs make a huge difference in the offer price that you receive. In addition to the items found in the inspection report, we recommend that you look at the following:

- **Curb Appeal/Lawn Care** - This is the first thing that the Buyers will see at your property, so you want to make the best first impression. Be sure the lawn is clean and free of debris. Focus on improving the landscape. You want a well-groomed property; add plants, flowers, and shrubs if needed to add to the curb appeal. If you have a deck/fence, consider fixing any missing boards, painting the fences, and staining the decks. Remove dead trees and foliage as needed.
- **House Exterior** - Look at the house paint and siding and make sure it leaves a positive impression. Power-wash the siding, consider replacing missing shingles on the roof, clean the gutters, etc.
- **Interior Paint** - We have become professional painters when it comes to simple jobs. We have even recruited friends and family in helping us with painting houses. We recommend light and neutral colors, which will make the home look brighter and larger. Prioritize the rooms that need to be painted. Paint is one of the

simpler tasks, yet can be time-consuming, so plan ahead.

- **Flooring** - We have learned the hard way that bad flooring will turn off Buyers and will affect their offer pricing. We have had real estate agents recommend that we simply hide issues with the carpets and/or not replace them, but we came to the realization that it sets the negative tone with the Buyers and pushes them toward more hardline negotiation. If the carpets or flooring are old/bad, examine your options. Maybe a good cleaning will work, or maybe you need to replace the flooring. If there's a hardwood floor underneath a soiled carpet and it's in good condition, you may want to pull the carpet up. Don't sink big money into this, but do your best to make sure not just the walls, but the flooring is appealing.
- **Kitchen** - Buyers know that they spend a lot of time in the kitchen, so you should closely examine the appliances. Can you clean them up to improve appearances? Do they need replacing? What about the paint in the kitchen, the floorboards, the cabinets? What can be done to make them look good with limited budgets? Also, look up to the ceiling. Is it stained? Are the cooking vents greasy? Don't forget to examine the lighting too. It's easy, especially in the kitchen, for lighting to attract flying insects that die within lighting fixtures if they aren't sealed off. It can be very unappealing to see dead flies there, so make sure this isn't the case.
- **Bathrooms** - Clean bathrooms are most important to Buyers. Ensure that all the toilets/faucets are in working order and not leaking. Take a look at the grout—if not clean, see if you can clean up or replace it. If you find loose tiles, see if you can fix them. If the linoleum

flooring is bad, consider replacing it. Check the flooring around the toilet for weakness indicating rot. If the toilet seat is old and unappealing, replace it.

- **Bedrooms** - If the bedrooms have old wallpaper, or dated/funky colors and patterns, consider removing the wallpaper and painting the walls a light color. This will make the room look larger and brighter. Our recommendation is to focus on the master bedroom first. Make sure the curtains are not too dark either. If the shades or vertical blinds are discolored or cracked, replace them.

- **Windows** - Typically Buyers are concerned about the windows and their condition due to the fact that old windows will affect the heating bill. If you're not replacing the windows, ensure they are clean, painted if needed, and there are no broken or foggy window panes. If you have broken or foggy windows, they will become an issue during inspections that you will have to negotiate.

- **Pets** - If you have pets, you will need to take special care to ensure that odors are addressed and that stained areas are taken care of. If you have a kitty litter box, make sure it is clean and remove it, if possible, before showings. If your Buyer is allergic to pets or they have concerns over pets, this could impact a Buyer's interest in your property.

COUPLES' ACTION SUMMARY

You have lived in your house and have a good idea of the issues that you face on a day-to-day basis in your home. The issues that you're aware of, may not be the same issues that a home inspector would find. It is important for us that you go through the process to do a deep dive on your house to identify any possible issues. Over the years, we have had our inspections done by a certified inspector, and at other times (for our rental properties), we have had them done by a general contractor that we had lined up. Regardless of the approach, it is important that you talk through together, as a team, how to develop your punch list of all that is needed to accomplish in order to get your house ready to sell.

1. Have pre-inspection done; ask friends/family/real estate agents for their recommendations
2. Go over issues revealed in pre-inspection
3. Line up contractors for repairs, if needed
4. Clean windows; lighten rooms (carpeting, walls, etc.)
5. If you have pets, eliminate any pet odors
6. Go over the budget if repairs are needed; determine what will be completed prior to listing property

It is important to note that different inspectors may find different issues in the property. However, we have found that inspectors follow a common process and the major issues are typically identified to help you determine how to best address and plan for a quick sale and negotiation strategy. Make sure you pick a good and reputable home inspector.

One of the things that is fun for us, and we have gotten good at, is painting. If you plan to sell your house early enough and have time to plan some of the activities together, painting can be a fun project that brings you closer while working together.

NOTES

NOTES

TASKS

Listing Your Home: Options and Considerations, By Owner or With an Agent

Carefully consider your own level of experience in real estate transactions.

Statistics are not on the side of For Sale By Owner (FSBO).

Real estate transactions are complex and require understanding the laws.

Negotiation skills are crucial for the success of a real estate transaction.

Bear in mind you can always negotiate on the commission amount.

VALUE OF TIME AND UNDERSTANDING THE RULES

MARKETING

REALTOR	FSBO
Access to MLS and experience in marketing houses	Buy access to MLS and will need to learn all aspects of marketing

DEDICATE TIME/ SHOWING EXPERIENCE

REALTOR	FSBO
Full time dedication and experienced salesperson	You may have a day time job; sales experience is preferred

NEGOTIATION OPTIONS AND PROCESS

REALTOR	FSBO
Experienced in dealing with issues; access to broker for support	Learn on the job; you will run into many issues that will require in order experience to resolve quickly

LEGAL PROCESS

REALTOR	FSBO
Licensed with a firm understanding of laws	May not have a full understanding of the local laws

MARKET PRICING

REALTOR	FSBO
Leverages tools and market data through a process; experience in pricing and addressing issues to get your price	Emotional ties with house; you will need to do full market analysis; may not price improvements correctly

LOCAL MARKET UNDERSTANDING

REALTOR	FSBO
Understands how the different communities in your area are selling and the type of Buyers in the area	Your view may be limited to your own community

CHAPTER SEVEN

LISTING YOUR HOME: OPTIONS AND CONSIDERATIONS, BY OWNER OR WITH AN AGENT

The decision whether to hire or not to hire a real estate agent is one of the critical decisions that you will have to make and it will affect the whole process.

- You need to consider your experience in real estate transactions
- Statistics are not on the side of For Sale By Owner (FSBO)
- Real estate transactions are complex and require an understanding of the real estate laws and contract procedures
- Negotiation skills are crucial for the success of a real estate transaction
- Keep in mind you can always negotiate the commission amount
- Saving money on commission is only one variable to consider, given that time and final sale value of your property have value too
- Regardless which way you decide to list, you need to do research to understand the market not only in your neighborhood but also in all surrounding neighborhoods

VALUE OF TIME AND UNDERSTANDING THE RULES GIVES YOU AN EDGE

Selling your house involves lots of time investments in getting the property ready and your family prepared to move. Your decision on how to list will affect the whole process.

YOUR OPTIONS

Listing your property is all about marketing your property, showing your property, working through offers, and finally going through the final process to close the deal. Choosing the right approach and team can affect the speed of how long it will take to sell your home, as well as the money you will make on the sale of it. Some of your decision options include:

- **For Sale By Owner (FSBO)** - The homeowner (you), as the Seller, will list the house without the assistance of a professional real estate agent. By going this route, you will be looking to avoid paying the listing agent/agency fees (typically 4%-6%). A number of services, including online, can help market the property. However, all marketing, showings, and negotiations will have to be overseen by you as the Seller.
- **Full Service Real Estate Agent with Fee** - This is listing with a professional real estate agent/agency who will support you in the full process. This includes a commission/fee on the sale of the property (typically 4%-6%).
- **Partial Service Real Agent with Fixed Fee** - A number of real estate companies have started to provide a fixed fee on the listing of your property, as well as options on other commission strategies that you can offer, to

help market and sell your house. You need to truly understand the offering as well as the services that you will receive for the discount, since this may require you to do quite a bit of work on your end. (This option may not be available with some agencies and is generally unpopular.)

WHAT IS THE MULTIPLE LISTING SERVICE (MLS) AND WHY DO I NEED IT?

In simple terms, the MLS is a central location in which real estate agents input their listings to share information about properties for sale. It is mainly a marketing and collaboration tool to share information, and helps Buyers and Sellers find available properties. The MLS is the primary database that the online services and realtors use to find out baseline information about properties for sale. It is important to note that the general public can't post listings into the MLS. Access to the MLS database is limited to licensed agents and brokers who pay for membership.

The main advantage of having your property listed on the MLS is the marketing and exposure that you will get by having more agents and Buyers knowing that your property is available for sale. In our experience, listing your property on the MLS brings a lot more Buyers to look at your property.

HOW DOES COMMISSION WORK IN TRADITIONAL REAL ESTATE TRANSACTION

When you hire a professional real estate agent - whether exclusively as the listing agent or a fee based agent - to help you sell your house, part of the agreement is the determination of the commission. The commission is paid by you, the Seller, and not the Buyer, when the property transfers ownership. In our experience, and we have used it time and time again, the commission is part of the negotiation when selecting a real estate agent, and the type of market will drive your negotiation power.

In a Seller's market when properties are moving fast, you'll have more room to negotiate than in a Buyer's market when there are many properties on the market that are not selling fast. In a Seller's market the homes are on the market longer and they will require more effort from the Seller's agent and therefore you may not have a lot of room to negotiate on the commission. Keep in mind, however, that the percentage of commission to sell a home is typically between 4-6% unless the home is very high priced. Listing a property at a commission rate that is too low can deter selling agents from showing your property to their Buyers. That is because commissions are typically shared/split between the Seller's agent and the Buyer's agent.

Additionally, even when split, the real estate agent involved in the sale will not be getting the full percentage that is agreed on. That is because it is also shared between the principal broker (person responsible for running the real estate office) and the agent. When negotiating the commission, it has been our experience that the principal broker in a real estate office has the final say. If you have ever bought a car, and you're dealing with a floor agent, every time the sales person needs to make a decision on pricing, they need to check with their sales manager. The principal broker plays a similar role for a real estate agent.

Depending on the market and value of your house, commissions are part of the hiring and selection process of a real estate agent. Some Sellers often wonder why a commission rate can't be lower, but bear in mind that this commission percentage covers inclusion in the MLS, advertising, staging, open houses, showings, being present at inspections, negotiating, preparing contracts, and more.

WHAT IS INVOLVED IN THE HOME SALE PROCESS?

In our experience, the home sales process is often oversimplified, it is not as simple as listing the property in the online boards, and showing the property, then signing the contract to close.

The home sales process involves several activities and decisions, including:

- At what price should I list my house?
- What are Buyers looking for, and getting house ready to list
- What marketing should be done, as well as listing/ photos etc.
- Should I stage?
- Running open house
- Showing the property
- Negotiating offers
- Accepting offers and coordination with contracts
- Dealing with inspections and post-inspection negotiation
- Negotiations to finalize and close the deal

We have also discovered that different states have different rules, regulations, and forms plus Buyers and Sellers have different rights across different states. If you do not have the expertise in these areas, you should consider contracting with an experienced real estate professional to represent and support you. If you do decide to still sell on your own, you may need to hire the assistance of an attorney and/or title company.

CONSIDERATIONS: BUYERS/SELLER MARKET

Differing market conditions can affect your decision on how to list. As we mentioned earlier, in a Seller's market, Buyers are ready to buy; they can't find the right house to purchase because houses are selling as fast as they are listed. You, as the Seller, could put your house up For Sale By Owner and you would have Buyers reaching out to you. If Buyers reach out to you with a real estate agent, you need to consider if you're willing to work with both Buyers with agents as well as Buyers without agents and develop negotiation. Additionally, you will need to draft a contract that will protect you, especially if you're dealing with a person that does not have an agent too

You will need to know what clauses you'll want to include in the contract. Additionally, you will need to develop an approach for qualifying Buyers as well as a plan to negotiate through the inspection process. Based on our experience and discussions with folks who have tried to sell properties on their own, difficulties can arise. Many times the deals fell through for one reason or another.

In a Buyer's market, it's the opposite. The inventory is high, meaning there are many properties on the market. The odds of a real estate agent bringing their Buyers to your property is lower. They have a lot of options for their Buyers and they want to ensure they get their commission. Most of your Buyers will be Buyers without an agent. You have to be willing to manage the negotiations, develop a strategy to price it right, and plan for low offers. You will need to consider more advertising and more showings. In addition, if you're in a Buyer's market and decided to sell it by yourself (FSBO), you may need to change your strategy if your house does not sell and you're not getting the traffic that is needed to your property. In this case, you may need to change your strategy and agree to pay the Buyer's real estate agent commission. Your only savings will be the commission you would have paid to the Seller's (your) agent.

RECOMMENDATION: USE A PROFESSIONAL REAL ESTATE AGENT

Unless you have sold a large number of properties and have a real estate or legal background, our firm recommendation is to contract with a professional real estate agent to represent and assist you in the sale of your home. With all the transactions that we have been through over the years, we have bought and sold both with an agent and without an agent. Today, we only do our transactions through an agent. The number of issues and challenges that comes with the real estate transactions vary, but having someone on your side who has the full understanding of the options, laws, and especially negotiation approaches to close the deal may mean the difference in closing the deal or having a deal fall through.

The main site that we have leveraged heavily to understand the market, whether it be through our own real estate activity or, more recently while gathering research for this book, is Zillow (www.zillow.com). The site contains interesting statistics that reinforce our recommendation to always list your property with a licensed real estate agent/agency. According to Zillow research (published 2020), 36% of Sellers attempt to sell their homes themselves, but challenges along the way lead many of them to eventually hire an agent. In the end, only 11% of Sellers end up selling their home without a real estate agent.

In the end, you need to follow the path that you believe works best for you. Our goal, as always, is to provide you with information based on our experiences, which can assist you in making the right decision when it comes to selling your house.

COUPLES' ACTION SUMMARY

For us, we both lead very busy lives that require us to balance both family and work. After going through the large number of real estate transactions that we have gone through and the number of contracts and renovations we have done over the years, we have learned that shortcuts and not leveraging the right expertise/help comes at a cost. It all depends on the cost you're willing to pay and invest in.

Looking at your backgrounds and experiences coupled with your time and availability that you can invest into selling your house can help you in your decision process in selling your house.

1. Understand the different options for selling
2. See the benefits of listing with a licensed real estate agent
3. Research the credentials of agents and agencies
4. Understand commissions, MLS, and selling the process

Depending on how far ahead you plan the activities to selling your house, the type of market conditions can help in your decision making process.

An additional factor that we take into consideration is how much equity we have in our house. That is, what is our mortgage or how much we owe on the house and roughly what we can sell the house for based on what sold in our area? If we can understand that and assume 6% commission on the property, we can understand our bottom line. Can we push the price up above the offer price to cover the commission? What is the value of our time? Are we willing to try a different approach because we have time and it is a Buyer's market? We truly recommend having these discussions as a couple as part of your decision-making process.

NOTES

NOTES

TASKS

☐

☐

☐

☐

☐

☐

☐

☐

☐

Selecting Your Agent

Not all real estate agents are the same; experience and connections will make a huge difference in the sale of your house.

- *You are in control; take the time to select the right team.*
- *Your agent needs to be a truly dynamic salesperson.*
- *The real estate agency that you go with is just as important as the real estate agent.*
- *Past sales records are a strong indicator of future potential.*
- *Real estate agents make a living off the sales commission.*

10 QUESTIONS TO ASK YOUR REALTOR

1. How many homes did you sell last year as a Seller's agent?
2. Of the homes you sold last year, as a Seller's agent, what was the average number of days from the original listing to the accepted offer?
3. Did you win any sales awards or get top listing or selling agent recognition over the past 2 years?
4. Can you list the components of your approach to marketing, and name your top five marketing priorities?
5. What was the typical difference or % between the listing price and the final selling price over the past 2 years?

6. What is your typical communication plan with Sellers and Buyers?
7. What is the action plan if we are not getting any showings?
8. Can you provide three customer references and three agent references in which you were the listing agent?
9. When a Buyer calls regarding my house will you ALWAYS be the one they communicate with?
10. How will you verify that the Buyer is qualified to purchase my home? What parameters do you look for?

CHAPTER EIGHT

SELECTING YOUR AGENT

Not all real estate agents are the same; experience and connections will make a huge difference in the sale of your house.

- You are in control; take the time to select the right team
- Your agent needs to be a truly good salesperson
- The real estate agency that you go with is just as important as the real estate agent you select
- Past sales record is an indicator of the future potential
- Look at facts and go with your gut feelings
- Ask the tough questions upfront
- Real estate agents make a living off the sales commission
- Real Estate agents are about selling; beware of the upfront sales pressures
- Selling your house is all about negotiation with the Buyer; terms, approach, and understanding needs
- It's important to take emotions out of the process: it is a business transaction for the parties involved

EXPERIENCE MATTERS

You would not hire an inexperienced mechanic to fix major issues in your car, so why would you hire an inexperienced agent to sell your house? Especially with high odds, they will cost the same.

EXPERIENCE MATTERS

Due to the number of challenges that we have had with inexperienced agents, along with the deals that fell through and the pain and struggles we've experienced, we encourage you to invest the time in selecting an agent that is experienced and dedicated to being an agent. Buying and selling real estate is about negotiation and being a great salesperson. Simply put, your real estate agent needs to have experience in dealing with real estate, along with strong negotiating skills to close the deal.

At the same time, we truly understand that everyone needs a chance to learn and succeed. You have to make the decision if you want to work with a junior agent vs. a senior agent, especially when the cost to hire either will most likely be the same (you typically pay the same commission). If you get a break in commission, then you need to consider if you are willing to invest the time/effort. In any market, your deal will go through or fail based on the negotiating skills and communication approaches between you and the Buyer. An experienced sales agent will help make this process easier.

Working with the right agent who understands your market, has the experience, understands your needs and thoughts, and, most importantly, can also negotiate on your behalf, is what all Sellers should strive for when they decide to list their home with a real estate agent/agency.

YOU ARE IN CONTROL; TAKE THE EMOTIONS OUT WHEN SELECTING AN AGENT

Over the years, we have given in to the pressures of either hiring a family friend who is a real estate agent, or going with the agent who has picked up the phone when we called the real estate office.

Agents who are related to you, or are friends of family, might not want to counter your opinions or ideas, even if it's in your best interest for them to do so. You might not feel comfortable demanding what you deserve, as you would with an agent who is not family or a friend. You need an agent you'll be able to interact with and work with one-on-one. You need an agent who can develop a relationship with a Buyer's agent to better understand what will be needed to close the deal.

If you go with a family member/friend and things do not go well, you could destroy your close relationship. If the family member/friend is experienced and you can honestly communicate back and forth without emotion, and you would like to consider them as your agent, you should have the conversation and establish rules upfront. If you both can understand your goals, and discuss future actions to accomplish them, including agreeing what to do if something goes wrong, then giving a family member or friend the opportunity to represent you in the listing and sale of your house can be an option. However, take the necessary time to think this through, and make a sound decision based on facts and confidence that you will be able to work with them. Letting them do so based solely on an emotional pull to do so, or feeling obligated to let them represent you in the sale of your home, is strongly discouraged.

HIRE THE COMPANY WITH WIDE EXPERIENCE AND A GREAT REPUTATION IN THE AREA

Do not underestimate the value of the real estate company that you use to list your property. When we discussed commission earlier, we explained that the principal broker (sales manager) represents the company and makes final decisions. A cut of every commission goes to the real estate agency that the agent works for. Think of the agent who is selling your house as your sales and marketing agent. The real estate agency itself covers costs associated with the services provided to sell your home. This includes advertising, staging, MLS listing, administrative staff costs, etc.

As an example, when selling one of our properties, we had options on what company we wanted to use. In that area, a builder was constructing a number of new homes, and the major real estate agent representing the builder (a local real estate agency) had a lot of listings in our neighborhood. When looking at options to list the house, we chose to go with another company. Over the next couple of months, most of the properties listed with the agent supporting the builder sold, while properties with other agents were not moving fast.

Later on we met with that agent over a cup of coffee to better understand what was going on. Her broker represented a couple of builders in the area. She explained that when potential Buyers came to look at new builds, they were able to network with the Buyer's agent, understand the Buyer's needs, and show their other listings across the area as options for Buyers, too. The broker of that agency was truly a good salesperson, and she pushed the marketing of the properties. We also took a look at some of the marketing packages produced by that agency, and it was a "WOW" compared to the marketing packages produced by the agent we went with. That was a lesson learned! It's important to understand not only what agent you work with, but the reasons you may want to consider the #1 local real estate agency to list your property. In many cases, as in this, they have the network to bring in more Buyers to look at your property and get it sold.

HIRE A SALES/MARKETING PERSON FIRST, AGENT SECOND

The selection process for selling a house is very different from the process for selecting an agent to buy a home. Think of the agent who is selling your house as your sales and marketing agent, not just a person with experience in selling a house. For instance, we worked with an agent who used to be a high school principal. After retiring, she decided to become a real estate agent. She had only been doing this for a couple of years, yet her success/track record was impressive. One of the key and interesting traits about her was her ability to listen, and respond effectively. She had the ability to negotiate through the issues. Her experience with dealing with people, coupled with the understanding of the processes involved in selling a house, were great.

Additionally, we truly believe part of her success was having a great team (agency) she worked for. From the very beginning, when dealing with us, her exceptional qualities and great team were evident. She and her team represent, as an "agent" should, the Seller in the most effective and professional way, while keeping the Buyers happy and interested as well. Although a listing agent represents the Seller, if the agent listens intently to what both the Seller and Buyer have to say during showings and negotiating, and they are backed up with a great team, they have the ability to sell the house in the most timely, effective and professional way.

HIRE A SALESPERSON WITH LOCAL MARKETING EXPERIENCE

When you are picking a real estate agent to work with, it is critical to check how they market homes online. It is important to ask the agent for some of their current or past listings. You should then look at the listings on sites like realtor.com and zillow.com to see how they are showcased. By doing so, you can determine if they write compelling real estate descriptions, if their photos are professional, and if they showcase the property well. Do the photos flow nicely, as if they are showing the exterior or interior well? Do they only have a couple pictures of the house, or did they take the time to photograph every aspect to showcase its features? Did they stage the property well when taking the photographs? Did they list important features that would attract a Buyer in the listing details? Your goal is to find an agent with great marketing skills who will know how to get the most out of your home's online listing.

In addition, do you see their name advertised in places? Do you know if they are involved in the community? It is important that the agent you choose to represent you is familiar with the area where your house is. Do they advertise regularly in the newspaper?

Ask your friends and neighbors about a listing agent you may be considering. Is their name familiar? If so, ask them how they know about them. An agent with local marketing experience will know how to get themselves known to Buyers. They will make sure their business cards are in local establishments, that they advertise in the paper and online, and that they are involved in some ways within the community they market in. They will represent their properties in the most professional way, too. Their listing packets, advertisements, etc. will be appealing to potential Buyers.

YOU ARE THE HIRING MANAGER - INTERVIEW AT LEAST THREE AGENTS/COMPANIES.

Please note that your questions for interviewing three agents/companies need to be geared to their experience as a Seller's agent, not a Buyer's agent, because they will be representing you, the Seller. The questions below are some of our typical questions we ask when we interview a Seller's agent to represent us. We try to work the questions into our conversations and interaction with the agents as part of the process.

For us, we make it a point to have the agent come meet us one-on-one. Preferably, we have the agent walk through the property we are selling. They will need to see the property to create a CMA

(Comparative Market Analysis) to show us what the suggested range for listing the property is in the current real estate market.

Our initial questions during this visit help us narrow down the list of agents we want to further consider to talk with face-to-face. We recommend this process for at least three agents. Although it can be time consuming, and it may be hard to say no to the agents not selected, it is important that you bring in the right team to help support you in selling your home. The CMAs you receive from these 3+ agents will also give you a good idea of what value is placed on your home. Each agent may have different results based on the comparative properties they use in the report.

Recommended Core Questions (Top 5)

- **How many homes did you sell last year as a Seller's agent, and have you received any top producer awards over the past two-three years?** You want a listing agent who has a track record of success in good markets, as well as bad. The agent's prior track record is the true measure of experience, not how many years he/she has been an agent. That is why we typically ask to work with the top Sellers in a given agency. You are looking for an agent who has sold at least 10 houses in the last 1-2 years, the more the better. If someone does not have the sales and claims they will work hard for you, know that the person with the track record will do the same and can back it up with proven sales. In addition, you will not pay more for the experienced person because it is typically the same commission you will pay to list your house with an agency.
- **Of the homes you sold in the last two years, again as a Seller's agent, what was the average number of days from the original list price to the accepted offer, and what was the typical difference or % between the listing price and the final selling price?** You want

a Realtor who understands the time it takes to sell a house on the market. In a Buyer's market, it is harder to sell your house and the odds are that the house will be on the market for a while. In a Seller's market it will sell faster but you want to maximize your returns. An agent that has experience in both markets is a plus. Additionally, the difference between the listed price and final offer can also be an indicator of the ability of your agent helping you in pricing your property correctly.

- **What is your approach to marketing, and how do you measure if the marketing is working? Also, can you provide me links to your current or previous listings?** You want a listing agent who has a systematic approach to marketing, and one who can provide you multiple options on marketing packages and projected plans. Additionally you want an agent who can talk about marketing beyond the listing, virtual tours, open house and print and online publications. You should be able to gauge if the sales agent can represent you well; asking about their current or previous listings is relevant. By getting a link to these listings, you will be able to see how long the property has been on the market, or, if sold, how long it was on the market before selling. This will give an idea on how effective their market efforts have been. Marketing in the most consistent and ongoing manner will be key, especially when putting a home up for sale with an agent in a Buyer's market.
- **Can you provide three customer and/or Buyer's agent references in which you were the listing and Seller agent in the past 2 years?** For us we ask these reference questions not necessarily with plans to call them, but to better gauge how the agent will respond to our question.

- **Will you allow me to terminate the listing contract if I am not completely satisfied?** One thing to remember is that an agent only makes a commission if they are able to sell your house. The question is for you to understand your options, and see how the agent responds to this tough question. You want to be fair in your working with the agent, but if you're not happy, you want to be able to talk to the broker to address any issues and, if necessary, you want to have the fair flexibility to replace the agent and/or move to a different agency.

Additional questions you may want to ask

- How will you communicate with us regarding your efforts?
- How will you verify that the Buyer is qualified to purchase my home?
- When a Buyer calls about my home, will you ALWAYS be the one communicating with the potential Buyer?
- What are your thoughts on staging, and what approach do you recommend?
- What is the action plan if we are not getting any showings? Can you tell me about a situation where you weren't getting any showings, and how did you resolve it and turn it around?

You may have additional questions, but the goal is to ensure you're comfortable with the real estate agent who will represent you when selling your house.

COUPLES' ACTION SUMMARY

We've tried to highlight the importance of finding the right real estate agent to support you in selling your house. Over the years, we have worked with a large number of agents on both sides of the fence, on the Seller's and Buyer's sides. When we look to purchase properties, as Buyers we can gauge if we can negotiate on a property by looking at the time and investment a real estate agent has taken into the marketing and listing of the property. If we do not see a lot of effort, we know that most probably we can negotiate on the property. Additionally a lot of times we call the listing agent directly if we have not decided to go with an agent yet, and from asking them questions on the property we can gauge/plan our approach. The listing agent will make a large difference in selling the property.

1. Before choosing an agent to represent you in the listing of your home, check their credentials and the details/track record of their agency. Make sure they will market the property well, and have good results as a Seller's agent. Take the time to interview at least three agents before deciding on who will list and represent your property.

2. Know the reasons, in the correct order, as to why you are hiring an agent to represent you; utilize this criteria when deciding whom you will hire.

3. Be aware of your emotions and don't let them be the drivers for your decision; this is a business deal.

We truly believe that in the end, choosing the right agent should be a joint effort. You will have to make a decision on the person that you will be working with throughout the process and that you will be entrusting the sale of your home. This is an important decision that can affect how stressful your selling process can be, especially in a Buyer's market.

NOTES

NOTES

TASKS

Pricing Strategies and Coordination with Agent

Do your homework. In the end you will have to accept and live with the final deal.

- *The market (supply/demand) will drive the final price of your house.*
- *You need to re-examine your price range with your agent.*
- *You should leave room in the original listing price for negotiation.*
- *Buyers like deals; like when purchasing a car, Buyers like to negotiate.*
- *It is possible to get your price while making a Buyer happy.*
- *Know that suggested repairs and proper staging of your house are to your benefit.*
- *It is common to go back and forth several times with counter-offers.*

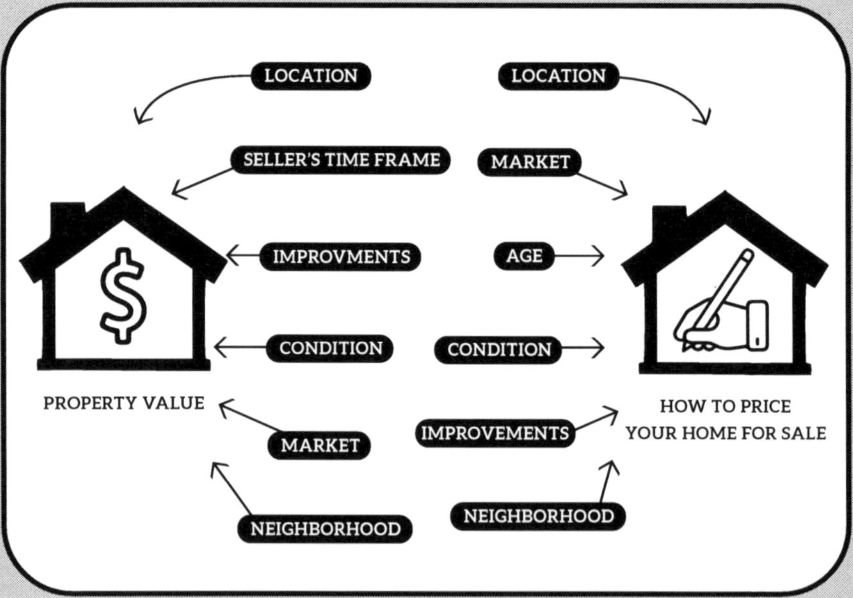

CHAPTER NINE

PRICING STRATEGIES AND COORDINATION WITH AGENT

Do your homework! In the end you have to accept and live with the deal; getting the right price is an important factor in selling.

- The market (supply/demand) will drive the final price of your house.
- You need to re-examine your price range with your agent. There can be differences between your desired target price and the Comparative Market Value (CMA) report you will receive from your agent. Keep an open mind while discussing the list price of your property. Although you may feel your house is more valuable than the CMA concludes, you have emotions that come into play with your thoughts on what your house is worth. By listing a price above a CMA price suggestion, you could have your house overpriced in the market, and this could dissuade potential Buyers from even looking at your home.
- You should leave room in the original price for negotiation.
- Buyers like deals, like when buying a car; Buyers like to negotiate.
- It is possible to get your price, as well as make the Buyer happy with the price they are offering.
- Know that suggested repairs and proper staging of your house are to your benefit so that you can bring attention to your house and get the highest price for it.

- Don't shut down a reasonable offer on your house simply because you feel the offer is too low. Many Buyers are just trying to feel the Seller out, and are trying to find the bottom line of the price the Seller will accept. It is common to go back and forth several times with counter-offers before a purchase contract is agreed to by both the Seller and Buyer.

LEAVE ROOM FOR NEGOTIATION

Pricing your house has to take into account that you will negotiate on price. Leave room for negotiating so it can be a "win-win" decision, with you getting the price you want, and the Buyer feeling like they've gotten a good deal. If you're lucky and get multiple competitive bids, you may get the listing price (or higher) as the final price you sell your house. .

THE MARKET DETERMINES THE VALUE OF YOUR HOUSE, YOUR PRICE IS THE STARTING POINT FOR NEGOTIATIONS

By understanding your bottom line and where you need to be, you can start planning and developing the terms of the negotiations. If in a Seller's Market, you may end up negotiating higher than your listing price, especially if you receive multiple offers. If in a Buyer's market, it will most likely be lower than your listing price. Remember, there are also contingencies linked to the asking price you may need to consider. A cash offer will usually close faster than one that requires a mortgage and because it is not subject to being approved for financing, could come in lower than one where a mortgage is needed. An offer where the Buyer needs to sell their home to purchase yours can be quite lengthy and may even fall through. The highest price offered is not always the best offer to accept. Carefully review and think through all the facts involved in any offer, even a full price offer or one higher than full price.

CMA VS. HOME APPRAISAL

A Comparative Market Value (CMA) is a report that is generated by taking a few similar recently sold (and sometimes not sold, but listed) properties in the vicinity of the subject property to compare and determine what the market value is for the subject property. This is usually done by a real estate agent to determine what they feel the listing price should be to sell the home. Features that are compared include size of land, square footage of property, number of bedrooms and bathrooms, proximity to subject property, age of house, etc. No one goes to inspect the homes being compared. Rather, the information is taken from the multiple listing system (MLS).

A home appraisal is more thorough. It will also compare similar properties, but will, in addition, go through the subject property thoroughly, evaluating repairs needed, as well as improvements made that might alter the price and come to a different conclusion than the CMA. The appraisal is always ordered by a bank/institution when providing financing for the Buyer. If the Buyer chooses to have a bank appraisal for information purposes, it can help determine how much financing can be made on the property (usually 80% of the purchase price for conventional financing). If a home appraisal comes in lower than needed for the Buyer, by having the financing contingency specified within the Purchase and Sale Agreement, this leaves the sale open to more negotiations and if a new agreement is not reached, it allows the Buyer to opt out of the sale since they are unable to finance it for the price they originally offered.

Both a CMA and a home appraisal can be very helpful in not only listing your property, but also in assuring you that your price is within the current market value and your house will appraise at a price that will qualify for a mortgage with a lending institution.

SET YOUR PRICING BOUNDARIES AND KEEP THEM CLOSE TO YOU

By understanding the bottom line price that you will accept as an offer on your home, you can start planning and developing the terms of the negotiations right away. This will help you when/if someone offers a lower price to purchase your home. You will know what your criteria is and therefore be able to keep negotiations moving forward in the most efficient and quickest way. It is important that you keep your lowest acceptable number private. In our experience, when people are hungry to make a deal and want to push it forward, information may be shared even when it is not expected to be shared. That being said, you can work with the CMAs as long as they fall in line with your numbers and if needed you know your bottom line. Another reason to keep your bottom line private is that you may change your mind based on different life events and/or number of offers/market conditions. This will allow you to keep your options open.

UNDERSTAND THE DIFFERENT INTERESTS IN THE PARTIES INVOLVED

Regardless of the environment we currently live in, in the end, your house is a business transaction for a lot of the parties involved in making the deal happen. A reminder that most parties will not get paid unless the sale of the house closes. Therefore, be cautious that different interested parties don't try to persuade you to take an offer that is not in your best interest. We will say, "Seller Beware." You should be an informed Seller and know what you want or need to get for your house. While you may decide to make some concessions to your original plan, you need to feel comfortable with the decisions you make.

In 2019, CJ's close relatives decided to sell their house, and they asked us to help them in selling it. They insisted on using a family friend who was a real estate agent, but not an experienced full-time agent. The agent was giving them a great deal on the commission listing 4% vs traditional 6%.

The first challenge that we had was agreeing on the listing value of the property. The agent lived far from the property and wanted to price it below the market value by $40K. In CJ's discussions with the agent, he felt not only was the agent new to this type of work, but the broker was driven by a desire to demonstrate an ability to move properties quickly. (CJ felt like he was talking to a wholesale car salesperson, they were all about moving larger inventory.)

The main reason for the pricing was the condition of the property. The relatives had not decluttered the house. Additionally, through the help of the agent, they had a contractor provide estimates for basic renovations which came to $25-30K in needed repairs, including painting, plumbing, hauling, etc. The agent indicated the low price was justified due to the condition of the house, even though all the homes recently sold in the area, as provided in the agent's CMA, were $30-40K higher.

CJ used tools on sites such as Zillow.com to get a general estimate based on the sold properties in the area. The estimate was closer to $40K higher than the recommended list price by the agent. The relatives had recently renovated the kitchen and basement which added value. In the end, CJ made the decision to delay the listing. CJ flew up to the area, coordinated to declutter the house, and got contractors to do the minor fixes needed; the budget for all the work was $5K. The major focus for improvements was on the bedrooms and bathrooms, as well as the curb appeal. In addition, CJ wrote the listing verbiage and coordinated the overall marketing approach. The property was then listed at $5K below the lowest recent sale in the neighborhood. Working closely with the agent through the process to sell the house, the house sold at $30K above the original suggested listing price recommended by the agent, a price delta of an extra $25K after all the negotiations!

All that being said, the agent was hungry and did a lot of work to support the sale. We could not have done it without the agent since we were helping remotely. On our end, we were able to follow our process to get the house ready, so that the agent could maximize the return. Given that CJ was not from the area in which the property was located, working with the agent was a great help. The agent was invaluable in running the open house, understanding the local laws, and working through the contract and closing process. CJ could not have done it alone.

Over the years, we have helped many acquaintances deal with real estate situations. The majority of the time, there are simple issues concerning the experience, sales skills, agency policies, and approach of the agent, as was the case in this situation.

GET THE PRICE RIGHT AND THE REST WILL FALL INTO PLACE

Pricing a house right regardless of market, coupled with the right listing information, is what brings in Buyers. It is important to understand that when Buyers are looking to purchase a home, they work within their own budgets. The pricing of your property will bring in the Buyer to at least take a look, either by going through the listing online or by wanting to pass by and physically take a walk through the property.

In our personal searches to buy a property, whether we are doing our own online searches or working with an agent, we always provide a price range for the property we are looking for. Understanding the pricing and the price range of houses that are similar to yours, will help you in setting a price that will have Buyers looking at your property.

LEAVE ROOM TO NEGOTIATE

All Buyers are looking for a deal. You need to leave enough room to allow a prospective Buyer to negotiate with you. Most Buyers want to believe that they got a deal when purchasing a home. Over the years, we have learned that we have to create the "win-win" situation to allow us to work through deals and issues that are found during the inspections. Depending on the market, we may be willing to negotiate differently. Regardless of the market, our goal is to have multiple offers and hopefully to work with the most qualified Buyers. This does not always mean it is the person who submits the highest offer.

We have made it a policy that we should expect the Buyers to submit an offer below the listing price. Based on the market and value of the property, we typically allow room for $5-10K of negotiations.

REVIEW AND UNDERSTAND THE LOCAL COMPETITION

Set your price in line with the local competition. You want Buyers to come to your house. You should go through the other houses for sale in your neighborhood. Ask your agent to walk you through them, and attend any local open houses. A clear comprehension of what else is available will help you in understanding how others looking at houses in your neighborhood will view your house.

We always say, you need to understand your competition and not just rely on your agent to understand the market. We believe in working closely with our agent as partners who will always take proactive steps in supporting moving the sale of our house forward. In our early days, we used to feel awkward about going to other open houses and walking through other houses for sale that were competing with our property. When we look back now, we realize that it is the smart thing to do, as we need to understand the local competition. We know that we are just being proactive and taking the steps to compete on the sale. Likewise, we cannot stop another person and/or their agent from viewing our property in order to position their property to compete with ours.

While looking at other properties for sale in your area, it is also a good idea to make note of the features that make yours stand out among the others. Is it located on a corner lot or at the end of a quiet street? Does it have a big deck or a large porch? These are just examples of some of the features that could attract a Buyer. Be sure to share these findings with your agent so they can use some of these stand-out features in the MLS and any advertisements for the property.

We strongly recommend you invest time to understand your competition. You also may need to be willing to lower the price to be able to compete and attract the right Buyer. We also understand that each house will ultimately have only one Buyer, so if the market is good, and you can understand how to compete, all you need is that one Buyer.

TIMING—PRICE YOUR HOUSE BASED ON SHIFTS IN THE MARKET

Your agent can provide you a better sense of how pricing fluctuates in your neighborhood. You may want to understand that as part of your plan for when to list the property. Additionally, this may also give you an understanding of when homes sell faster or for a higher price in your neighborhood.

In our experience, you'll have Buyers looking at different times of the year for different reasons. Additionally you will have different people listing properties at different times of the year. We have further come to realize that different areas have higher demands at different times of year, and that your price point will need to take into account the high and low seasons for your local area.

In general, many Sellers list in the spring and early summer because people are making plans for a move and want to relocate prior to the start of the next school year. The market tends to slow down in some areas during the winter months because of holidays and, in some areas, weather reasons.

For us, in the areas that we invest, we typically aim to buy in the winter seasons. Less inventory coupled with a lower number of people looking can create a Buyer's market in an area that is typically a Seller's market. We have seen that we typically have a lot more room to negotiate on price. When we sell, we like to list in April/May, the beginning of spring, and/or toward the end of summer before school season, since we have found that is the time when the market starts transitioning to a Seller's market and we can make a greater profit on the sale of our property. Again, we recommend that you develop an understanding of your own market and the time you plan to list your property in order to help support your pricing objectives.

SET YOUR PRICE BASED ON AN ANALYSIS AND FINANCIAL NEEDS

Selling your house is never an easy process, especially if you have lived in the house and raised a family in it. A lot of people can get emotionally attached to their house, and that emotional attachment affects their judgement when valuing a home. In addition, you may have invested in fixing the property over the years to address issues that may not be reflected in the price. You may have had to deal with major plumbing or foundation issues that were not expected and cost a lot of money. This may not be reflected in the market pricing, and you may not be able to recoup as much as you want in the sale of the house. One of our acquaintances had bought a house for her daughter during college, and her daughter had roommates. After the daughter graduated, the house was rented to college students for a number of years. The students did a lot of damage to the house which required a lot of work on the walls, carpets, and bathrooms, as well as the outside landscaping. These all had to be addressed in order for the house to be on par with other houses on the market, especially since it was a Buyer's market. The owner was so emotionally stressed with the house and the amount of money spent. In the end she had to decide if she wanted to invest in getting the house to compete in the market, or if she should take it off the market and wait. It was a rough journey to a state of acceptance that many of the renovation costs that had been done through the years would not be recovered, and that she needed to price the house according to market conditions.

WORK CLOSELY WITH YOUR AGENT, AND DEVELOP A STRATEGY

We have mentioned that you are in control of your process, and hiring the right agent is key to help you succeed. If you decide to work with an agent, it is important to work closely together as a team. Your agent will prepare a CMA for you. Together, you can discuss the suggested listing price generated by this report and come to an agreement on what price your house should be listed at. The strategy that you develop for pricing the house will vary depending on whether it is a Seller's market or a Buyer's market. In either case, it is important to understand your options and approach for pricing.

As a team, you can also discuss the marketing steps the agent has planned for you. Discussing any concerns potential Buyers have after a showing can quickly address what may need to be done to resolve them. Always know that this is your house and, although you have hired someone to represent you, it is important to stay involved in the process in ways that can be helpful to get a sale. After all, who knows your house better than you do?

COUPLES' ACTION SUMMARY

You truly have to be realistic and understand your local market in order to price your house tight. A lot of market drivers affect how your Buyers will be able to afford to pay the asking price.

Pricing your house will start with you working together as a couple to understand your finances and what is needed. When we talk about what is needed, you need to understand what is owed on your current property and what options you will need to consider as part of your next phase/chapter of your lives. Oftentimes, it may not be an option to buy a new house contingent on the sale of your current house, especially if you're trying to move into an area that is a Seller's market. You may need to consider interim transitions such as a short-term rental or renting for a year. Simple things to consider:

1. Price the property right, leave room for negotiations
2. Highlight your special features
3. Know your competition and understand the current market
4. Work together as a team with your agent.

We have used the opportunity of moving from one house to another, selling our home vs. selling an investment property, to actually help us establish better financial stability for our family. We have been lucky that we have made decisions around the market conditions and did not buy high. Furthermore, we lived in each house for at least 5 years, during which time the housing market improved and we developed equity in the house. We have used some of the funds of the sale of the houses to pay off a college loan as well as pay off credit card debit, using some of the funds to invest into college funds for our kids.

Regardless if you're in a Seller's or Buyer's market, take the steps to maximize your returns and generate equity to help build financial stability into your future.

NOTES

NOTES

TASKS

Action Plan with Agent

Now that you have selected an agent, it is important to have an agreed-upon approach.

- *Strong and clear communication is critical.*
- *Manage expectations and develop trust in each other*
- *Your plan may differ based on the market you're in (Seller's Market vs. Buyers Market).*
- *Establish timelines and key target dates.*
- *Identify the closing team.*
- *Identify contractors that can support you at the time of inspection findings.*
- *Finalize pricing.*
- *Establish a marketing approach.*
- *Re-examine your next steps and move.*
- *Clearly document your understanding and verbal agreements.*

THE HIGH-LEVEL ACTION PLAN - THE KICK-OFF

1. Do an initial walk-through of the house with your agent.
2. Review the listings in your area.
3. Visit Open House events with your agent.
4. Review any additional recommendations for minor renovations.
5. Plan your staging approach.
6. Review CMA and develop pricing strategy.
7. Establish Marketing plan and strategy.
8. Plan for Realtor and Buyer Open Houses.
9. Identify contractors that can assist you.
10. Establish a schedule and timelines.

CHAPTER TEN

ACTION PLAN WITH AGENT

Now that you have selected an agent, it is important to have an agreed upon approach and have your support team ready.

- Communication is Key
- Manage expectations and develop trust
- Your plan may differ based on the market (Seller's Market vs. Buyer's Market)
- Establish timelines and target dates
- Identify the closing team
- Identify contractors that can support you at the time of inspection findings
- Finalize pricing
- Establish an approach to marketing
- Re-examine your next steps and move
- Document your understanding and verbal agreements

KICKSTART THE SALES PROCESS

Now that you have selected an agent, it is important to develop the coordinated action plan and allow the real estate agent to become your sales agent.

ESTABLISH COMMUNICATION APPROACH

It is important to have trust between you and your agent. The first step in doing so is to establish a positive and clear communication approach. Some of our recommendations include:

- **Understand and communicate why you're selling** - Be ready to communicate why you are selling, and define your needs and goals. It is important that the agent you're working with understands the drivers behind selling your house.
- **Ask the questions** - Do not feel that asking your agent too many questions, or even just one question which might have an obvious answer, may make you sound like you do not understand the process. Ask the questions that are on your mind; your agent's job is to help you and this will also build trust relationships between you and your agent. It is important that you ask and discuss needed questions to help you make the right decisions.
- **Transparency is key** - Once you sign an agreement with your agent, he or she has the legal obligation to represent your interests in all negotiations. Your agent also has the responsibility to be fair and honest with prospective Buyers. You can request your agent keep certain things private. As a licensed professional, your agent is aware of the responsibility to not disclose information that is not required by law.
- **Get Clarifications, do not take immediate positions** - Based on his/her experience and training, an agent will provide recommendations on your approach. If you're unhappy or not sure about something, we strongly recommend you take the time to better understand why that position is being taken. Take the time to ask leading questions and/or have an open discussion on how to best

address your concerns. Not discussing the issues that you have questions about may cause more challenges down the road, and may cause trust issues to develop between you and your agent.

- **Establishing communication channels and schedules** - Discuss with your agent the best ways to reach each other. In addition, establish mechanisms and approaches for communicating. As an example, you can establish a 12/24 hour policy. If you do not hear back within 12/24 hours, decide what the next step will be to escalate a response. Discuss work hours, schedules, backup contacts, and best times to reach each other. Maybe even set up planned touchpoints. We have realized that when working with agents, reaching them by phone is rarely the best option. We have moved to text and email communication as a main medium after initial meetings. Connecting through texts or emails allows the agents to communicate with you even when they are in other showings etc. Good agents will typically respond right away and let you know when they will be able to respond to you by phone, in more detail, etc.
- **Establishing Showing Protocols** - It is widely recommended that when an agent is showing the property, the owner of the property is not present. We tend to agree with this. Again, your house is very personal to you. Your emotional side should not be part of the showing and can be a deterrent for both Buyer and Seller. At times, your agent may not even be present unless it is during an open house, although, if you prefer them to be, you can make that a stipulation in the listing agreement with them. If you are still living in the house, you need to work closely with your agent to establish times when an agent can bring potential Buyers to look at the property. The potential

Buyer will want to go through every room in the house, including bathrooms, bedrooms, kitchen, etc. You need to have those rooms/areas ready for potential Buyers to walk through. You also need to agree to times and protocols for impromptu showings. If a clear protocol is not established, this can add tremendous stress to the process. Worse, it can lose you an interested Buyer.

- **Seller's vs. Buyer's market considerations** - We have talked about Seller and Buyer markets. It is important that you communicate and discuss with your agent the market conditions, along with some of the expected challenges. You should also discuss approaches and potential challenges such that you have a high level of agreement on what is to be expected.

THE HIGH-LEVEL ACTION PLAN -THE KICK-OFF

We have discussed the overall sales process. The action plan now is all about how to get the house ready, finalizing the listing price, establishing the marketing approach, getting your contractor ready, and going through the motions of managing the offers. At this stage of the process, the plan assumes that you have already gone through the process of decluttering, have done your pre-inspection and addressed any major findings, performed minor renovations, and have worked on curb appeal. If you have followed most of the steps, it will make the next step of working with your agent much easier. At this stage, we recommend planning through the open house. It is assumed you have had the discussions about potential offers and next steps, but mainly you want to be focused on planning to get the house on the market, see what types of offers can be anticipated, and then adjust your approach as needed.

- **The walk-through** - Do an initial walk-through the house with your agent. During the walk-through, you should take notes for recommendations for each and every room. Even though you have already gone through, decluttered, and made the minor renovations yourself, your real estate agent will bring in a different perspective, from a salesperson's view, with new recommendations. In our experience, if the house is decluttered and in semi-ready shape, the agent will have a better view of other recommendations that may be needed to prepare your house for the market and showcasing it in the best possible way. Make sure you document the recommendations during this walk-through so that you can create an action list. Set an immediate action plan to address these recommendations so they will not greatly affect your timing and schedules.
- **Your house binder** - We have recommended you develop a home binder to share with your prospective Buyers. At this stage, we also recommend reviewing the binder with your agent and making decisions on what information would be good to add or remove, and how best to present it.
- **Neighborhood/open house listings** - Work with your agent to look at the current listings in your neighborhood/area. You can take a look at the online listings, and also ask the agent to take you for a walk-through of your top three competitors. By going through those listings, you can help develop an additional action list which will help you in the pricing, as well as staging discussions.
- **Staging discussion** - After the walk-through, you should have a discussion about staging with your agent and get his/her thoughts on this. Your discussions should also include how staging your property will

compare to other houses currently available for sale and/or sold in your area. Buyers will compare houses, if not by visiting them, then by looking at online photos and listing descriptions. Later in this book, we will have a more detailed discussion on staging your house and our recommendations.

- **CMA/Pricing strategy** - As discussed earlier, numerous factors affect the pricing of your home. You should have a discussion about the CMA results with your agent, as well as determine the pricing strategy, especially in a Buyer's market. Note any additional steps that will be needed to finalize the decisions.

- **Marketing steps and options review** - Marketing strategy is one of the most critical steps, and just as important as the pricing. Part of a successful action plan includes discussions on marketing, including taking photos of your house, as well as other logistics. The timing and scheduling of these activities will affect when your house will be listed on the market. We will have a more detailed discussion on marketing steps later in this book.

- **Open house planning** - We view the open house(s) for a property as a critical component of selling a house. In a Seller's market, if done right, it wouldn't be unusual for you to receive multiple offers. At the very least, you will be able to narrow down the list of interested parties for follow-up. In a Buyer's market, the open house becomes more critical, and we typically ask the agent to plan for multiple open houses upfront. It is important to have discussions with your agent about the open house. This will require schedule coordination on your side and the agent's side. In addition, your house needs to be ready prior to your open house so it shows in the best possible way. First impressions mean a lot!

- **The Contractors** - This is a lower priority at this stage, but start planning early to have professionals ready to support you in your estimates. If you do not have a general contractor that you typically work with, ask your agent if he/she would recommend any contractors. Most contractors plan out months ahead of time. If you wait too long to contact one when needed, you may find out there is none available to do any work required on your house prior to selling it.

THE SCHEDULE

Now that the high level action plan is in place, it is important to begin planning around your timeline, even scheduling specific dates. Developing a schedule for tasks and planned completion dates is an important aspect of the planning that can help you achieve your goals and priorities in the time you have available. This is especially important when you have to coordinate activities among multiple people. Additionally, this will help you better understand your dates and what you can realistically achieve within the time you meet with your agent until the time you plan to have the open house for your property.

Time is the one resource that moves fast, and you need to plan accordingly. Scheduling helps you plan your house sales effort by helping you work through what you want to achieve in a day, week or month. It will help you track your steps to accomplish your goals.

COUPLES' ACTION SUMMARY

Now that you have selected your agent, start working as a team to take the next steps. It is important when possible, especially in the initial meeting with your agent, for both of you to be present during the initial kick-off/planning meeting.

Some of the things to consider as part of your first meeting include:

1. Establishing a communication plan with your agent
2. Kicking off with a high level action plan
3. Determining a schedule to adhere to; planning accordingly

Through strategic planning, you can have your house in the best possible shape for your open house. First impressions mean the most, so make it a great one!

We strongly recommend that you talk with your agent about what the market/competition is like in your current area. You should have him/her look up numbers for you on local and neighboring listings so that you continue to develop an understanding of your competition. We strongly encourage you to schedule time to visit open houses as well as viewing local listings in your area, to help develop a baseline. Also take a look at the listing descriptions as well as the photos, and price your house so you can compete accordingly.

We also recommend that you do a second walk-through of your house. Finalize the action list for getting your house ready with the agent, talk about the staging options, the marketing options, and other recommended minor renovations. We strongly recommend that you review the market and develop an understanding of the market conditions of Seller's vs. Buyer's markets. Finally, discuss pricing strategy as well as how you're going to deal with the challenges especially if you're in a Buyer's market. If you're in a Seller's market, discuss options on how you can best maximize your returns.

NOTES

NOTES

TASKS

Getting the House Ready for the Beauty Contest

In the initial walk-through, you want your Buyer to imagine themselves living in your house. Because it is a contest between your house and other houses in the market, you need to do the best that you can to have it "show" ready.

- *You want to showcase a loved house.*
- *Curb appeal is key; first impressions are critical.*
- *Staging your house properly is extremely important.*
- *Focus on open-space concepts.*
- *Remember: every room counts.*
- *Organize, Organize, Organize.*
- *Add light and brighten your spaces.*

Let Your House Stand Out Among The Crowd

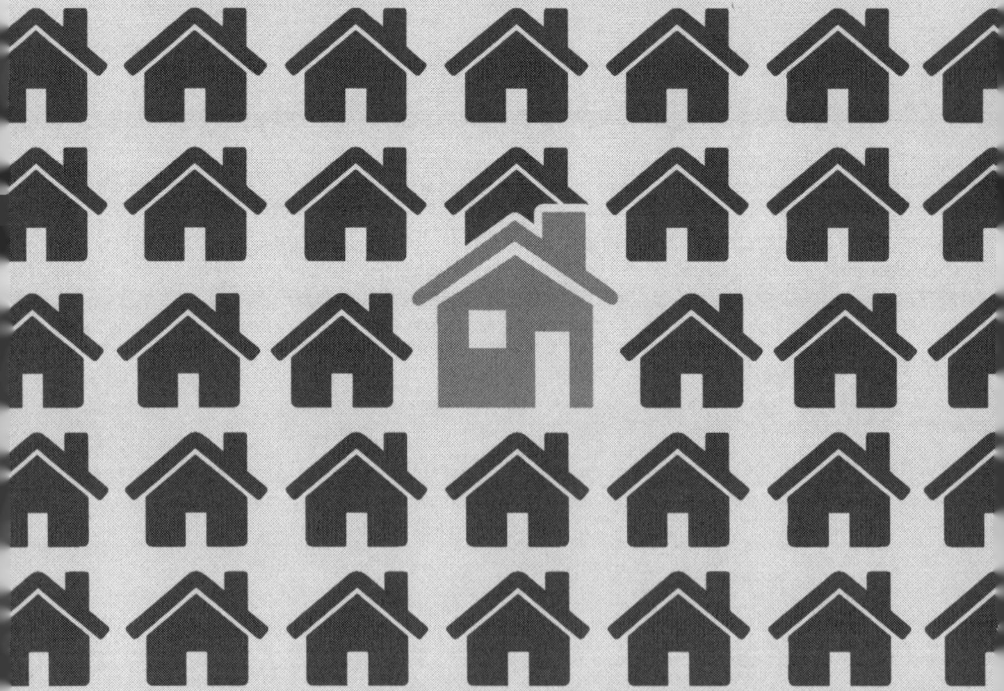

CHAPTER ELEVEN

GETTING THE HOUSE READY FOR THE BEAUTY CONTEST

In the initial walk-through, you want your Buyer to imagine themselves living in your house. You need to prep your house for sale. Because it is a contest between your house and other houses in the market, you need to do the best that you can and have it "show" ready.

- You want to showcase a loved house
- Buyers will look at a number of houses before making a decision; you want your house to stand out in the crowd
- Buyer's impression on the house will effect the offer price
- You want to showcase a loved house, and present a house that the buyer can visualize living in
- Curb appeal is key; first impressions are important
- Staging your house well is essential—make it professional
- Focus on open space concepts
- Buyers will want to walk through each room in the house; *every* room counts
- Organize, organize, organize and make the house stand out
- Adding light and brightening your spaces will help the rooms appear larger
- Focus on the key features of the house

MAKE THE FIRST IMPRESSION THE BEST IMPRESSION

Have your house "show" ready. Make it shine inside and out.

THE LOVED HOUSE: APPEAL TO YOUR BUYER'S IMAGINATION

When we were shopping for a new home for our family, one of the homes was smaller in size than what we were looking for, but it was the house that our kids wanted to buy. They kept on mentioning how nice it would be to live in that house. It was staged well, and in the open basement, they had a family table with a number of board games available. One of the board games was set up as if people were playing it. This caught the imagination of the kids and family. We actually talked about how much fun it would be to hang out in the basement to watch TV and play board games together. The objective of the stagers worked. If the property was larger, we would have made an offer, but it was a very hard decision to walk away. Plus, it gave us insight as to how to generate a desirable feeling in the staging process to appeal to Buyers.

How you get your house ready for your potential Buyers to walk through it is very important. You want to have every room in the house appealing and inviting, and set up in a way to capture the imagination of your potential Buyer, like the smaller home did to us.

THE CURB APPEAL

Curb appeal is how nice your property appears when looking at it from the street. As an example, the yard is well-kept, the paint is vibrant, the siding looks good, the roof is intact, and things are in order. In our experience, curb appeal sets expectations.

Prospective Buyers are more likely to want to look inside your house if they like what they see on the outside. You can think of the curb appeal as a marketing tool for your property.

First impressions make a difference when it comes to selling a home. At first glance, you want your property to have a "wow" factor and entice Buyers to want to come in and take a look inside. You can improve the curb appeal of your property in many different ways. When we were looking for a professional makeover for one of our properties, we wanted to use a local nursery, but scheduling a meeting took a very long time, and then the cost was higher than our budget. We decided to use a DIY Do-It-Yourself approach regarding landscaping. Time and cost are both factors to weigh when determining whether you will hire someone, or do-it-yourself, like we did.

Some of the considerations for your curb appeal may include:

- **Landscaping (Grass and Trees)** - Your curb appeal starts with the condition of the grass, trees, and landscaping of your property. Dead grass, bushes, and weeds all over the lawn may reflect a house that is not cared for, and Buyers may not want to see the inside thinking the interior will not be cared for either. Consider planting seeds and watering the yard for a few weeks, or you may want to consider sod. If you have overgrown or dying bushes, you should plan to trim or remove them. A fresh layer of mulch can completely transform a property's exterior. Drive around your neighborhood, look at houses that have great curb appeal, and see what you like that could also improve the curb appeal of your own property.
- **Driveway** - When Buyers are pulling into your property, they will either park or walk through the driveway to the entrance of your house. Driveways full of weeds or cracks do not send a good message to new Buyers.

- **Front Door** - Almost everyone will walk into your house through your front door. If it is worn out or dirty, consider painting or replacing it. A nice wreath or door ornament can make it more appealing and inviting.
- **Roof** - If the roof is old and has only a few years left, and/or it is worn out or has visible damage, it will definitely be one of the items discovered and noted in the home inspection. Consider a new roof or fixing to make it more appealing.
- **Exterior** - A dirty exterior is something that should be addressed. Power washing a deck or the siding is a good investment and isn't costly.

LIGHT - BRIGHTEN AND OPEN YOUR SPACES

It is important to consider the lighting of your home. The type of light bulbs you use in your rooms make a difference. Brighter bulbs give a better appearance. The color choice of your walls is also important. Using brighter light bulbs, opening up the shades and curtains, can make the room brighter and more inviting when the house is being shown. Other ideas for brightening and opening up your living space include:

- **Colors** - Use neutral colors on the walls; you can add color with furniture and decorations.
- **Decluttering** - Go through a second round of decluttering to create more open space and remove unnecessary items in the house that may distract the Buyers from really seeing the home.
- **Downsize** - Oversized furniture and home accessories can make a room feel smaller than it really is. A room that is overstuffed is going to feel cramped.

- **The Kitchen** - Remove items from the kitchen counters such as coffee makers, toasters, microwaves, etc. Look into options to make the kitchen an area where your potential Buyers will want to cook and share meals.

- **The Bathrooms** - Make sure that your bathroom is in good shape. You can also add accessories like fluffy towels and decorative pieces to make the space more inviting.

- **The Bedrooms** - The bedrooms are important. How clean they look, the appeal of the bedcovers, wall decor, curtains, and how organized the closets are will make a big difference on the Buyer's impression of the house. Be sure to show some open space within the closet areas also. Otherwise, they will appear smaller.

- **The Garage** - People often underestimate the value of a well- organized garage. People looking to get away from their cluttered environment, would love to see the garage potential in the new house.

- **Views** - If you have nice views, trees, lakes, etc., make sure you have your windows open, highlighting the landscape for potential Buyers. Also ensure your windows are clean.

- **Clean house** - Buyers like to see clean homes, even with fixer-uppers. A clean house can get you a better offer. A dirty house will give the wrong impression to Buyers.

Buyers can accept buying a house that needs some care and fixing, but we have seen that most Buyers prefer to buy something that's almost move-in-ready.

PROFESSIONAL STAGING VS DIY STAGING

To Stage or Not to Stage professionally? Good question, but we believe you should always stage because first impressions are lasting ones. We have come to the realization that staging makes a bigger difference in a Buyer's market, given that Buyers can be more choosy. In a Seller's market, properties are scarce and Buyers need to act on them as soon as possible, but staging can help bring in higher offers. In our definition, home staging is the process of getting your home ready for the sale, with a goal of making the home appealing to a wide range of potential Buyers. In staging your house, you add to the property's appeal, making it welcoming, so that a Buyer can envision himself or herself living there. This typically includes the use of art, painting, accessories, lights, greenery, and carpeting, to give potential Buyers a more attractive first impression of the property. This also may include rearranging or "temporarily replacing" furniture.

In general, staging is:

- **Going Beyond Decorating** - It's choosing the right props, moving or getting rid of furniture that makes the space look smaller, and creating focal points in main living areas.
- **Maximizing Your Space** - Beyond repainting and cleaning, staging a house aims at making it look bigger, brighter, and cleaner, and accentuating the positive aspects of the property. It's all about creating a sense of possibility and potential, about creating an inviting space to inspire Buyers to get attached to the house.

Leveraging a home staging professional, or deciding to do it yourself, will depend on your time, budget, and level of expertise. Here are some things to consider to help you make an informed decision:

Professional Home Staging

- **Professional Expertise** - Experienced home stagers bring in the experience of staging a house to sell, not only to make it look nice. They bring experience from working in this industry and knowing how to position each room to highlight specific features for the Buyer. Additionally, they bring an understanding of the real estate market as a whole and locally, as well as demographics and trends.
- **Saves time and stress** - Putting it in the hands of a professional saves your time and effort. Staging requires you going through each room and identifying what is needed for each room and how to do a makeover for each room, with an understanding of the appeal needed for potential Buyers. This will take a lot of time and effort that a professional stager can help you with.
- **Access to short Term Rental Furniture** - Professional home stagers have access to a wide range of inventory to decorate and/or do a makeover for your house. Little things will make a huge difference in helping the Buyer visualize this space as her/her new home. Professional stagers can provide a wide range of options that a homeowner would not typically have or think of placing in a given space.
- **Can work with your budgets/furniture** - Stagers can work with you on your budgets and approach, especially if your existing furniture can be leveraged to showcase your house. In addition, for a fee, some stagers may be willing to walk through your property and provide you recommendations.
- **Cost** - Home stagers typically charge for both their time and use of their furniture. In addition a home

stager will have time frames in which you can rent the furniture. If your home is on the market a long time, it may increase the cost.

DIY Home Staging

- **Market** – If you're in a Seller's market and your home is in good condition, you may want to consider getting multiple quotes and/or recommendations from staging experts, even if you are considering doing it yourself. By doing so you'll have a better sense of whether to do it yourself or hire a company. Additionally, by talking to multiple companies, you can receive ideas and recommendations that you can implement if you do ultimately attempt to stage yourself.
- **Time** - Consider looking at your schedule, and availability to help in getting your house ready.
- **Saving** - You can save money by doing the staging yourself. If you have to buy accessories/furniture, this may affect your overall savings.

General Staging Recommendations

- **Modern look** - Avoid a dated look such as old curtains; replace dated decor with something simple and neutral.
- **White Linens** - Switching shower curtains, towels, and bedding to white or light neutral colors can make a big difference in overall impression.
- **Maximize visual availability of storage** - You should have packed all non-essential items. Do one more round, go through your cabinets and closets and remove any items that are unnecessary.
- **Architectural Details** - Draw attention to any architectural details, like molding and large windows that you want your Buyer to notice.

- **Closets** - Organize the closets. Buyers will open closet doors. Make sure they don't see a big mess.
- **Scents** - Candles and air fresheners throughout the house can be helpful, if not of an overwhelming scent.

Our recommendation is to work with your agent to get their input and recommendations on staging. Then, meet one or two of the professional stagers they recommend in order to get an idea of what these stagers can offer you, while fully understanding your options.

COUPLES' ACTION SUMMARY

In our experience, this is the fun part of the journey, after you have put in a lot of time and effort to declutter, depersonalize, and perform minor renovations.

Now it is time to get your house ready for what we call the "beauty contest." In summary, we recommend that you go through the process of developing an action list coupled with target dates for when you would like to complete each action item. We recommend including the following items as part of your initial action lists:

- Give your house curb appeal.
- Brighten up your living space.
- Recognize the importance of staging, and respect and consider a qualified stager's expertise on what will bring in Buyers and higher offers on your home.
- Determine your budget for getting the property in "show" condition.

For us, this is part of the process in which we work as a team to divide and conquer. We also try to make it a fun activity for the both of us. As part of this process, your house is being transformed into your product that will help you secure the next step of your future. In our experience, it is important that you take an active part in the staging process of your house, that you have looked at the competition in your area and understand the options that your Buyers have, and, in addition to getting your house ready, you need to be able to plan through some of your options for the future as a couple.

Furthermore, we recommend you invite friends and family to and get additional feedback and recommendations. Take any feedback that fits your vision into account as part of your planning your next steps.

NOTES

NOTES

TASKS

The Listing, Marketing Plan, Open House, and Timing

The listing description is critical. Buyers typically read it even before looking at the photos and videos.

- *Marketing is the key to getting Buyers to take a look at your property.*
- *Effective marketing goes well beyond the listing.*
- *You need to ensure you have a follow-up process in place for interested Buyers.*
- *Buyers look at price, pictures, videos, the neighborhood, and listing descriptions.*
- *You want your pictures to tell a story and make your house stand out.*

The Marketing Plan - 10 Key Focus Areas

We recommend that you work closely with your agent on the marketing plan to establish a strategy for approach. Here are 10 recommended focus areas that we have leveraged or highly recommend based on our many lessons learned and also agent recommendations.

Your Target Audience Profile
It is important to consider who the potential Buyers will be for your house.

The Marketing Brochure
Throughout our interactions with a wide range of real estate agents, we have seen many basic, but also stunning brochures. We strongly recommend you stress the importance.

The MLS Listing
Be sure to devote plenty of time and thought to formulating the property description.

Coming Soon
Let the community and potential Buyers know about your house once it is about to come on the market.

The Community Binder
Highlight your community and neighborhood.

Local Real Estate Agents/Brokers Open House
Plan for an open house midweek for brokers and real estate agents. Cater a lunch, which could be as simple as pizza or subs.

Professional Photo Shoot
Great pictures are a critical marketing tool. Imagine yourself as the prospective Buyer and visualize yourself walking through the different rooms with the order and highlight of the pictures.

Aerial View/Video, Drones
Today, the use of Drones can provide a cost-effective way to take aerial video of your property.

Public Open House
The open house is an integral part of the process that will bring in Buyers to your house.

Online Real Estate Search Engines, and Your Local Community and Social Media
In addition to the traditional MLS listing, review and update sites such as Zillow.com.

CHAPTER TWELVE

THE LISTING, MARKETING PLAN, OPEN HOUSE, AND TIMING

The listing description is critical. Buyers typically read it before looking at the photos and videos.

- Marketing is the key to getting Buyers to take a look at your property.
- Effective marketing goes beyond the listing. Moving forward, marketing is an important component of everything you do to effectively sell your property.
- You need to market not only to attract Buyers to look at the property, but to ensure you have a follow-up process in place with interested Buyers.
- Buyers typically look at price, pictures, videos, the neighborhood, and your listing description to add your property to their short list of properties to see.
- You want your house pictures and images to tell a story, to make your house stand out, and to make the Buyers anxious to see it.
- With the time and effort invested in preparing the property, now is time to showcase and kickstart the process.

SHOWCASE YOUR HARD WORK

You have worked hard and invested a lot of time and effort in order to get your house ready. Marketing is your opportunity to showcase it and the starting point to getting your house sold.

ARE YOU A MOTIVATED SELLER WILLING TO MAKE A DEAL?

Have you noticed properties for sale where they state "motivated Seller", or have you heard of or known motivated Sellers? As Buyers, we typically look for motivated Sellers because we are looking for deals. As Sellers, we try to avoid the situation of being motivated Sellers. The phrase "motivated Seller" in real estate listings can mean a number of things. But primarily it means as a Seller (property owner), you're eager and willing to negotiate in order to sell your property quickly. The desire to close quickly can be for any number of reasons.

In the market, the term "motivated Seller" typically means the Seller is eager and may have some desperation associated with the sale. You may also request your agent to "tell Buyers you are motivated" for any number of reasons. We typically see this more in a Buyer's market than a Seller's market, but if you let your agent know that you're a motivated Seller, it usually means:

- You have room for negotiation on the price and are open to further price reductions.
- You're willing to make selling concessions for the Buyer. This may include different concessions on closing costs, as well as other terms based on inspection findings.
- You have pressures and you need to sell your house fast.
- You want to see offers and are willing to discuss numbers and entertain discussions before the official offer.

We mention "motivated Seller" in this section because it will help you determine how to support and drive your marketing approach. You need to decide if you are a motivated Seller and plan accordingly. We try to avoid becoming motivated Sellers by doing the proper planning upfront. Yes, we have been motivated

Sellers in the past, but we try to avoid it by managing our activities, timeline, and budget.

THE IMPORTANCE OF THE MARKETING PLAN

A property that we are selling needs to be highlighted properly in order for it to sell at the right price. Think of commercials or when you go to the grocery store; what prompts you to pick one product over the other? Quality, as well as the product look and feel and design, will make a huge difference in your selection process. Marketing is a huge driver in what you see. You have to think of your house in a similar manner and work closely with your agent to ensure these objectives are being met. The extent of your marketing to sell your property should never be merely posting your listing on the MLS, simple updates to the listing, and a few quick photos.

Returning to our recommendations on hiring a sales/marketing person first, realize that developing a marketing plan should not be a "one size fits all" approach. The marketing plan for each property needs to follow some general guidelines, but should also be tailored to the specific property based on several variables such as property condition, location, target audience, price range, and market conditions. It truly requires a knowledge of your target audience, as well as careful planning. As with any planning process, start by establishing goals and measurable objectives for your marketing plan. For example, a goal could be selling a listing at above market value, or selling the property within two months. Measurable objectives could include having a certain number of offers/inquiries after a marketing event, such as the open house.

Once your goals are in place, it's easy to next identify which marketing approach you should focus on in your plan. Having a target goal of measurable results allows you to make a decision or measure if your approach is working. As an example, if you have an open house, and you only have 1-2 people show up to the open house and none show interest in the property—while other properties in the neighborhood have traffic—you need to go back and carefully examine your marketing approach, as well as other possible factors, to see what could be done to generate and improve the interest on your home. We also recommend that you go back and do a deep dive on understanding your competition by revisiting their online listings, and get out to see the other properties. This will help you refine your strategy moving forward.

THE MARKETING PLAN - 10 KEY FOCUS AREAS

We recommend that you work closely with your agent on the marketing plan to establish a strong and clear strategy. Here are ten key focus areas that we have leveraged or highly recommend based on the lessons we have learned, plus recommendations from agents.

1. **Your Target Audience Profile** - When establishing your target audience, it is important to consider who the potential Buyers will be for your house. By looking at your current community and its trends, you can determine a profile of who has been buying homes in your neighborhood. Is your house in a retirement community? Is the neighborhood made up of mostly single people or retirees, or do young families and/or for relocating military families flock there? Different audiences will play differing factors in the range of marketing steps you should consider.

2. **The Community Binder** - Once you have identified your target audience profile, we recommend going back and looking at the community binder that you have been compiling and finalizing what is to be included in

it. Are there any additional items and features you could highlight? Work on organizing it in a way you would want potential Buyers to see it.

3. **Professional Photo Shoot** - We cannot underestimate the value of good pictures. Great pictures are a critical marketing tool, and you need to ensure that they are professional and showcase your house. The images can flow through a virtual walk-through. Imagine yourself as the prospective Buyer; visualize walking through the various rooms with the order and highlights of the pictures. Make sure the pictures capture areas you would specifically like highlighted. Pay close attention to how this walk-through would make you feel if you were a potential Buyer. These images and the virtual walk-through are what a prospective Buyer will examine in order to make the decision as to whether or not to add your house to their list of potential properties. It is truly the potential Buyer's first impression of the home. Interior photography and video can often be done by the same person, so getting these tasks completed together makes sense, saving you time as you proceed with your real estate listing marketing plan. The bottom line: Be sure that before you even think of posting the home on the MLS, your website, or social media, you have professional photos making the first impression.

4. **Aerial View/Video, Drones** - Most real estate agents offer aerial videos as part of the marketing package. Today, with the use of drones, they can provide a cost-effective way to take aerial video of your property. Aerial videos can showcase additional detail for Buyers, which can include:

    - Aerial views of entire property and surrounding land
    - A walk through the neighborhood

- Home and community amenities
- Property boundaries and exterior highlights

5. **The Marketing Brochure** - Throughout our interactions with a wide range of real estate agents, we have seen both very basic brochures, as well as quite stunning ones. We strongly recommend you stress the importance of creating a stunning brochure to your agent, and then make sure you get one. Again, great looking brochures shouldn't be complicated or expensive, but they should be of high quality and make for an impressive presentation.

6. **The MLS Listing** - In the next section, we will discuss the listing description in greater detail. But briefly, it is of critical importance that you dedicate time and much thought into formulating a compelling property description for your listing.The description needs to draw the reader in by highlighting the uniqueness of your house, in order to get Buyers to come see it.

7. **Coming Soon** - We think it is important to let the community and potential Buyers know about your house once it is about to come on the market. When potential Buyers are looking for a property in a given neighborhood, in addition to looking at planned listings, they will typically drive around the neighborhoods. We actually bought our second home after seeing a "Coming Soon" sign, and we were able to establish a relationship with the agent early on. Now we always ensure that we let the neighborhood community know early that our property will be for sale soon. This helps jumpstart and line up prospective Buyers.

8. **Local Real Estate Agents/Brokers Open House** - We recommend that part of your marketing is to plan for an open house midweek for brokers and real estate agents. Cater a lunch, which could be as simple as pizza or subs.

We strongly suggest that you do this first prior to the public open house. Here's why:

- It gives you access to the clients those real estate professionals represent. Each broker/agent who walks into your house may represent a number of potential Buyers. By going through the house, and getting to know your real estate agent and creating a relationship, they will get to know the features and layout of your house that may appeal to their potential Buyers.
- Create Demand - If agents see other agents interested in the property and they have Buyers that may be interested, they will indicate their interest and plan to coordinate showings quickly.
- Get initial feedback - Other agents will share their thoughts and opinions, as well as provide recommendations. This is valuable input that you can use to take action on as you get ready for the next stages of the process.

9. **Online Real Estate Search Engines, Your Local Community and Social Media** - In addition to the traditional MLS listing and the listings real estate agents provide to potential Buyers, many Buyers conduct their own market research online. Websites such as realtor.com, zillow.com, and trulia.com are available to the public and are easy to navigate, gaining additional information for Buyers. A site like zillow even allows the owner to add features and their own notes in the listing. Be sure to review your listing on these sites and provide feedback to your agent for any suggested revisions or improvements.
10. **Public Open House** - The open house is part of the process that will bring in Buyers to your house, and will give your agent the opportunity to talk to the potential

Buyers personally and in greater depth. At this stage, you want to be ready to provide the best impression possible.

- Ensure your house is staged
- Make sure your professional brochures are ready
- Advertise/Showcase your Open House effectively
- Plan the follow-up (sign up lists)

The above ten focus areas of your marketing plan and approach are things that we consider and take into account when working with our agents.Your agent should be flexible and work closely with you to measure the results and adjust your marketing approach accordingly. Note that when you're working with your agent on the marketing materials, if you see something you do not like or you want improved, you need to share your thoughts and options and then discuss potential solutions.

THE IMPORTANCE OF THE LISTING AND PROPERTY DESCRIPTION

The text on the listing is so important! How you list your property, and how you talk about your property, will be part of the first impression of your house, determining whether Buyers schedule a showing. Buyers on the market are reading multiple listings each day. To save time, they probably read the first few lines and skim through the rest of the content. They want to get the facts quickly so they can move on and determine what properties are worth paying more attention to. If the listing doesn't have what they're looking for, they will pass it by. If what they read is compelling, they will start looking at more information on the property, as well as the photos and videos. Even if the property isn't in their initial target range, if it is strongly appealing, they will take into consideration setting up a walk-through and may end up vying for your home.

- **Research** - Always look at properties with similar layout, rooms and neighborhoods. Read other listing descriptions; look at properties that sold to see what was inspirational or appealing in their property description; highlight what you like or don't like in each listing.
- **Be Concise** - Market research indicates that approximately 250 words is the optimal length for a property listing description. Aiim to capture your audience in the first couple of sentences. This brief description should integrate verbs/words that inspire imagination and generate interest.
- **Highlight features** - Highlight the top features, brands and reasons that make your house a great place to live. Aim for your listing to be engaging. Talk about the front porch as a place to enjoy a hot cup of coffee in the morning, or the large kitchen as the perfect space for entertaining.

We'll close with an example of one of our own listings, which prompted numerous interested Buyers to reach out:

Location! Location!!! Great location inside the beltway! Close to 66, Rt. 7, 123, Tysons and convenient to WFC and the new Tysons Corner metro. Great neighborhood with excellent schools! Spacious SFH in move-in condition with open floor plan and big fenced backyard. Nice front porch, 5 BR and 3 FB. Home has been recently remodeled and updated with built-in ceiling lights and gleaming Brazilian cherry hardwood floors throughout most of the main level. Kitchen has been completely remodeled and features ceramic floor, high end appliances, cherry cabinets with lazy susan, built-in wine rack and wine fridge, and beautiful granite countertops with a breakfast/bar area. Huge attic with custom built walk in closet and lots of storage. Large family room with a wood burning fireplace and sliding door overlooking a large fenced yard w/ outdoor patio, and children's play set. Mature fruit trees including pear, apricot and two amazing fig trees with plenty of delicious fruit. Perfect for your own garden and your family to enjoy!

COUPLES' ACTION SUMMARY

We have shared with you our recommendations regarding the importance of your marketing plan and approach. Again, you have done the hard work and effort to get your house ready. But until you showcase the house in a manner that attracts Buyers to want to look at your house and consider it as an option, you will not be able to maximize the value of all your efforts.

1. Be careful about representing yourself as a motivated Seller. Know the reasons why this can be a detriment in selling your home.
2. Establish and know your targeted areas well.
3. Review your binder. Make sure it is full of helpful and relevant information, and finalize it.
4. Remember, first impressions are lasting impressions. They determine whether a Buyer will show further interest in your home. Make sure the first impression of your house is the best it can be! Be sure to review all marketing material, including the MLS information.
5. Prepare for an Agent Open House.
6. Prepare for a Public Open House.
7. Give yourself a hand - you worked hard to prepare and now you are ready for offers to come in!

Your marketing objectives are to attract as many potential Buyers to create competition and multiple offers such that you have options. In order to develop a better understanding of your marketing objectives, you should schedule regular follow-up with your agent to discuss what feedback you have been getting and to see if any adjustments are needed based on initial feedback. Always keep an objective and a positive outlook on the feedback and determine what is the best approach to address any concerns.

NOTES

NOTES

TASKS

The Offer: Negotiation Strategies

When a Buyer decides to walk away, they only risk the earnest deposit that they provided you.

Your goal is to potentially have multiple offers. You need to ensure that you look at qualified offers only, and don't rush on your decisions.

The number of potential issues that can come up during the selling process are vast; you need to be willing to negotiate.

Try to understand the Buyer's needs and why they are purchasing your house. This will give you better leverage.

Trust your instincts and gut feelings. Don't dismiss your feelings if you sense something isn't right.

In general, you need to take emotions out of the equation as much as possible. Treat this as a business deal.

People tend to hold you to your promises, whether written or unwritten. Make sure you document, and communicate your commitments in writing.

When You May Want to Walk Away

DURING OFFER STAGE:

- The Buyer starts trying to lowball
- The Buyer doesn't properly put earnest funds forward

DURING APPRAISAL STAGE:

- The appraisal came back too low and the Buyer won't budge

DURING INSPECTION STAGE:

- Buyer Concession - The Buyer asks for numerous concessions and it gets out of hand

AT CLOSING STAGE:

- The Buyer pushes to change move date, or changes their needs and is willing to lose deposit

AT ANY STAGE:

- The Buyer threatens to walk away (more than once)
- Cold Feet - The obvious fear of the commitment on the Buyer's side

CHAPTER THIRTEEN

THE OFFER: NEGOTIATION STRATEGIES

When a Buyer decides to walk away, they only risk the earnest deposit that they provided you.

- Your goal is to have multiple offers; you need to ensure you look at qualified offers only, and don't rush any decisions—thoroughly read all offers because contingencies, financing capabilities, inspections, etc., are also very important in ensuring the offer you accept is a solid one and won't fall through.
- The number of potential issues during the selling process are vast; you need to be willing to negotiate; don't toss aside an offer simply because it is lower than what you want. Instead, counter-offer with your numbers (and sometimes a bit higher for further negotiations). Many times the Buyer is just feeling you out and is both willing and able to offer more or even meet your price.
- Try to understand the Buyer's needs and why they are purchasing your house. This will give you better leverage when negotiating, and knowing their needs and objectives will also let you know how serious they are about purchasing your home.
- Trust your instinct and gut feelings. If you feel something isn't right when a Buyer continues to ask for extensions on a contract, or promises that an offer is coming in but hasn't followed through yet, don't dismiss

that feeling. Although emotions need to be in order, a gut feeling or instinct can warn you when something isn't quite right.

- In general, you need to take the emotions out as much as possible. Treat this as a business deal. Showing your emotions to a Buyer can weaken your leverage during negotiations. If a Buyer sees you are desperate to sell, they will many times bring in a much lower offer than what they originally planned.
- People tend to hold you to your promises, written or unwritten. Make sure you document, and communicate your commitments in writing.

PATIENCE

Just because you receive an offer, does not mean you're going to close on the house. Focus on the highest quality offers.

BE WILLING TO WALK AWAY FROM THE OFFER/DEAL

You may need to walk away from a house negotiation. Even if you're desperate to sell, knowing when to walk away from a house negotiation can, in the long run, save you time, money, and tons of stress. The tricky part is understanding whether the Buyers you have are worth working with, or if it's better to walk away from a deal and start all over again. Your agent can help, but make sure they are thinking of your best interests rather than their own. Remember, agents only get paid when a sale comes through and many live on these means only.

Negotiation starts at the time of the offer. Examples of times when you need to consider walking away from the negotiation:

- **During Offer Stage**
  - Buyer keeps offering a lower price and Buyer's final offer is below the offer price you're willing to accept.
  - A Buyer doesn't give a good faith deposit, or offers one that is very low with their offer. This allows the Buyer to walk away any time due to the low deposit amount. This does not demonstrate their strong commitment to their offer.
- **During Appraisal Stage**
  - Appraisal came back too low and the price is below what you're willing to accept, or you may not have room if you accept the appraisal price. Know that you may still need to lower the price during the inspection process and you may need to establish negotiation parameters or walk away.
- **During Inspection Stage**
  - Buyer asks for too many concessions, and you're unable to agree on renovation list, concessions, and/or adding funds toward closing.
- **At Any Stage**
  - The Buyer more than once, has indicated if requests are not met, they will walk away.
  - Cold Feet - The obvious fear of the commitment on the Buyer's side indicates a risk that they may be willing to lose the deposit.

Take the time to choose the right offer upfront since the negotiations and process for closing on a fully executed purchase and sale agreement takes time.

THE IMPORTANCE OF SPECIFIC TERMS IN THE SALES CONTRACT

Key terms in the sales contract can give the Buyer some leverage throughout the sales process. You, as the Seller, need to be aware of these. In a traditional offer, the Buyer will position the contract in a manner that will provide them an advantage where possible. They want to position the contract so that they can walk away from it if necessary without losing their deposit(s). You, as the Seller, want to ensure that you are protected once you accept the offer and have the opportunity to work through the issues as they arise to keep the contract moving forward.

Below we present some sample scenarios with our thoughts. Please note that each situation is different, and you should consult with legal counsel and/or an experienced real estate agent when it comes to your own situation. The scenarios below are intended for you to discuss with your agent, and to help determine if additional terms should be included in your contract to allow you options. Different states will have different laws and clauses that should be considered with the guidance of your agent and/or legal advisor. Based on some of the scenarios mentioned below, you will see why we recommend a pre-inspection on your property. It will help you be prepared to deal with potential issues.

Scenario - Buyer's Offer has insufficient Earnest Money Deposit

- Example: The Earnest Money Deposit is the amount of money the Buyer will put down as part of the offer. It helps show the commitment of the Buyer to the offer. If the Buyer decides to walk away from the deal for no reason, the deposit belongs to the Seller. The Buyer submits an offer and the earnest deposit is low.

- Our thoughts: Simply put, you should not accept the offer when the earnest deposit is low. Depending on the market (Buyer's or Seller's), you will need to consider different options. In a Seller's market, depending on the number of offers, you can request an increase in the earnest deposit to help protect you. In a Buyer's market, you can still request an increase in the deposit but you need to be able to ensure your agent builds the relationship with the Buyer's agent, in order to request the increase. Even in a Buyer's market, if the earnest deposit is too low, we recommend you do not accept the offer.

Scenario - Financing Contingency

- Example: A financing contingency is a clause in a home purchase and sale agreement that expresses your offer is contingent on being able to secure financing for the house. Typically a Buyer uses this clause to establish a set period of time to apply for a mortgage and/or close on the loan. After going through the process and getting close to the closing date, the Buyer asks for an extension of the Financing Contingency.
- Our thoughts: In our experience, there are many situations where the problem is not the Buyer's fault. Perhaps the bank is requesting more information that takes time and it may be out of the control of the Buyer. If the Buyer has been supportive and easy to work with throughout the process, we recommend that you take the time to request from the Buyer to provide you the lender's stated final conditions for funding the loan. In looking at the information, you can work with your real estate agent to review the conditions to better understand the timeframes needed to close and you can

make a decision on the extension. In our experience, you need to put in place a reasonable and acceptable time to support the contingencies. If the Buyer is asking for a very lengthy time, you should present a counter-offer reducing the time, be willing to walk away, or take the risk.

Scenario - Home Sale Contingency

- Example: You received an offer with a home sale contingency, that the offer received from the Buyer is contingent on the Buyer selling their home. This means the Buyer wants to buy your house only if they can sell their current home. The Buyer has specified the timeframe (usually 30 to 60 days) to sell their home, or else the offer and contract for buying your house is voided.
- Our thoughts: Typically the most common reason for this type of offer is due to the fact that the Buyer does not qualify or does not want to carry two mortgages. Depending on the number of offers on the table, and the type of market, you need to consider your options. Accepting the contingency is a risk, because if the Buyer's home sale falls through for any reason, you have to go back to the beginning and restart the process of putting your house on the market. That being said, in either a Seller's or a Buyer's market, you need to understand what stage the Buyer is at in selling their home and decide on the level of risk you're willing to accept. Examples of Buyer's stages include:
    - **Listing** – The Buyer just started the process. Try to look at their listing and/or market area they are in, is the listing done well, are they in a Seller's or Buyer's market. Ask your agent to help get the information if needed.

- **Offer** – Does the Buyer have an offer pending? Is the contract signed?
- **Inspection Stage** - Inspection has been finalized and final negotiations based on findings are in process.
- **Closing** - If they are in the closing stage, determine if the closing date set/finalized based on inspection results.

Scenario - Major issue found during the home inspection

- <u>Example:</u> During the home inspection, major issues were revealed, such as structural damage to the floor joists and/or leaks in the roof. The Buyer wants to terminate the agreement, but you as a Seller are willing to make the repairs.
- <u>Our thoughts:</u> You should have your agent walk you through the inspection options and terms before signing the Purchase and Sale Agreement. From our experience, you should always have the inspection terms written in such a way that the Buyer can not just walk away if they are unhappy with the inspection. Instead, you, as the Seller, should have the option to address/fix the issue, and Buyer should not be able to simply walk away. Be sure to ask your agent or legal advisor how to review those terms of the offer.

Scenario - Buyer has indicated they want to pull out of deal for no reason (The importance of the earnest deposit)

- <u>Example:</u> Just when you think you're about to close on selling your house, the Buyer indicates that they are no longer interested in the property and just wants to walk away. You had multiple offers, but chose this Buyer. The process was long and time-consuming and you worked through appraisals and inspections. But now you will have to start all over.

- Our Thoughts: We have learned the hard way that sometimes Buyers decide to walk away from deals and may not give you a reason. At times they will try to negotiate getting back the earnest deposit. From our experience, once you accept the offer, the key term that will keep the Buyer from walking away for no reason is the risk of losing the earnest deposit. The deposit is your (Seller's) protection to ensure that the Buyer will go through with the commitments of the contract. In our experience, if you have included the terms to allow you to negotiate, you need to ensure that the earnest deposit will cover your cost for 2-4 months or the time spent in having your property for sale. You need to have the terms in place to prevent the Buyer walking away from the offer for no reason.

Scenario - The Importance of Disclosures

- Example: In our last house, we discovered a foundation issue in the basement during pre-inspection, prior to the sale of the house. The foundation issue was due to water coming from behind the wall, and it was causing a crack. Should we address it prior to listing the property, or do we disclose it in the listing?

- Our Thoughts: In our experience, and we live by this policy, "honesty is the best policy." We want to be treated fairly, and we want to treat others fairly in our dealings. If we are aware of an issue, it is our responsibility to address it. We have faced situations like this when an issue was found that was expensive to resolve. In this case, we addressed it and had to account for it in our price. It was a tough option for us. It was expensive to resolve and we did not have the funds to cover the cost of repairs. We opted to hire a foundation specialist and had them repair the crack. We had the information about the reason for the crack and the repair done on it available. The repair was visual, and we knew the Buyer's inspector would identify the issue. We did lose a number of potential Buyers due to this—they did not submit offers. But still one Buyer went through the process and asked to talk with the company that did the repair. The sale of the house was more challenging, but we had taken the extra steps to make the house look great, show it was loved, and we were able to find the right Buyer. We truly believe that the fact we disclosed the issue upfront and had the right paperwork allowed us to win the confidence of the Buyer. We were able to get through the full process and close with only one offer.

DEALING WITH MULTIPLE OFFERS

For the majority of the houses we have sold, we have had to address the issue of multiple offers. This is a good problem to have! In our experience, it is not always the highest priced offer that is the best offer. You truly need to look at a number of variables in the selection and qualifying process. Your agent is there to help you with this. They will point out the parts in the contract that are most significant. The decision on what offer to choose, however, is yours.

You will need to take into account

- Pre-Qualifications letter
- Employment status of offeror
- Reason for the Buyer wanting to buy the house
- Earnest deposit amount
- Contract escalation terms - Does the Buyer have terms in the contract to give them options for when to close?
- Contract terms based on inspection - are they offering you the option to address issues or not?
- Contingencies that the Buyer has added to the contract.
- Will the Buyer require financing or is it a cash offer?
- Does the Buyer need to sell their own home before they can purchase yours?

Be aware that there things that are prohibited from being taken into account by the Seller and/or their Agent due to the Federal Fair Housing Act of 1968 and the Federal Fair Housing Act Amendment of 1988. To name some, decisions based on:

- Race or Color
- Religion
- National Origin
- Familial Status or Age
- Disability or Handicap
- Sex

YOU'RE NOT DONE UNTIL YOU CLOSE; THE DEAL CAN FALL APART AT ANY STAGE

Early on in our real estate journey, we used to assume that once we had the signed offer by both parties we were all set—the deal was done! Today we are fully aware that the deal is not done until we sign the papers at closing. If you ask any real estate professional who has been in the business even a short time, they will tell you that there are no guarantees. A deal can fall through at any time. How you manage the deal and negotiations will determine if you're going to be able to save the deal or simply walk away from it.

THE IMPORTANCE OF THE ORIGINAL OFFER DEPOSIT AMOUNT - UNDERSTAND WHEN A BUYER CAN WALK AWAY

Buyers want to position the offer so that they can walk away when possible with minimal cost. It is the job of the Buyer's agent to negotiate the best terms for the Buyer.

- The Buyer may still be looking at other properties while waiting to see the results of the inspection after the offer. If they see a property they like more, they may be willing to forgo the deposit or use a strategy of making a high number of demands based on the inspection report in order to forcc you to release them from their obligation.
- The Buyer may have financial obligations and they need to find a way to walk away. The wife of one of our friends lost her job after they had submitted an offer and it was accepted. They had to walk away, due to the financial risk. It was not the fault of the Seller. We know of others who had a death in the family that triggered them walking away. In both instances, they negotiated with the Seller and the Seller accepted partial payment

of the original deposit. The clauses in the contract protected the Seller and forced the negotiation on the table.

- The Buyer may not be happy with some of the findings in the inspection report. You want them to give you the option to address the findings, rather than just walking away.

It is important that the Buyer puts down a sum of money as part of the deposit such that it makes them think twice about walking away. The type of market (Seller's or Buyer's) can drive this amount; for example, in a Seller's market you can increase your demand to reduce your risk of the Buyer walking away.

Talk to your agent and ensure you develop an understanding, given normal conditions, of when a Buyer can walk away without losing their deposit. Those are areas of focus.

UNDERSTAND THE BUYER'S NEEDS, THEN ADJUST DURING NEGOTIATION

If you have a Buyer who is fully qualified and truly interested in your property, work with your agent to develop a better understanding of the Buyer's needs/objectives, to help determine if you can negotiate your way through.

When you talk to agents, the story they always tell is Buyers and Sellers should not communicate directly because the agents are best positioned to negotiate. It is their job. We would agree with this to an extent. But in our experience, you are in charge in the final deal, and you need to be provided enough information to understand the concerns and situations of the Buyer to allow you to provide recommendations and/or concessions on your end—some of which may be out-of-the box ideas—to facilitate the deal going through. It goes back to our original position: you are the person that is ultimately in charge and you get to define the decision-making process.

COUPLES' ACTION SUMMARY

Negotiations on your house sale can stretch on throughout the entire escrow process, and you may find issues and disagreements coming out of the woodwork. If you're concerned that the deal may be turning sour, the best thing you can do is consult your real estate agent. Your agent knows the market in your area better than anyone else and will be the best adviser throughout the entire process. Remember, don't let your emotions rule, because emotions can change in an instant. Instead, look at everything in a constructive way, determining whether ongoing issues can be resolved in a mutually agreeable way or if they just aren't worth carrying forward with.

1. Review qualified offers thoroughly and take your time doing so.
2. Understand the importance of deposits and why a Buyer should be willing to put down enough of a deposit that will encourage them to work through a deal if situations arise, rather than walk away and waste your time.
3. Be prepared for multiple offers and stay calm when you receive them. Again, take your time reviewing them and read them thoroughly; have your agent go over the strengths and weaknesses; remember that even the strongest offers can still be negotiated.
4. Understand the steps involved once your house goes under contract with a Buyer.
5. Know what could go wrong in the process.
6. Know the warning signs as to when to consider walking away from a deal.
7. Know the Buyer's needs in purchasing the home.

NOTES

TASKS

The Appraisal, Inspection Reports, and Negotiation Strategies

Pre-inspection of your property will make the process easier by reducing the number of surprises.

This is the area with the highest risk of the contract falling through, due to issues found iduring inspections and the negotiation process.

Take the emotions out and focus on this as a business deal.

At this stage, you as the Seller need to plan to negotiate and grant concessions to the Buyer to close the deal.

This is a negotiation; it will go back and forth. You need to to be patient and willing to let your agent help manage this process.

Understand that this is one of the more stressful periods for both the Buyer and Seller. Focus on win-win strategies.

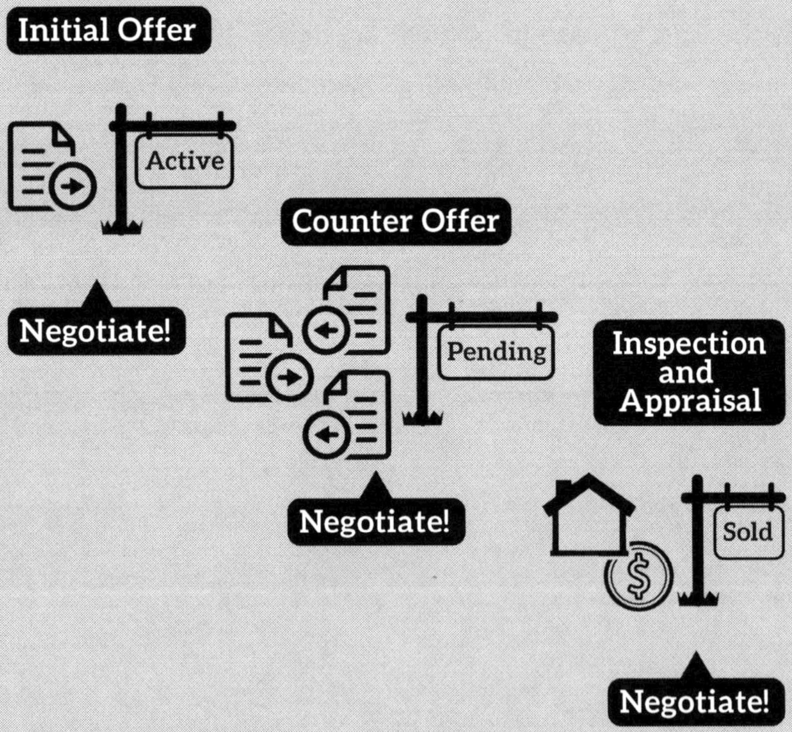

CHAPTER FOURTEEN

THE APPRAISAL, INSPECTION REPORTS, AND NEGOTIATION STRATEGIES

To get the deal closed, the appraisal and inspections are areas that you need to pay close attention to and be ready to negotiate.

- This chapter will reinforce our recommendation: be sure to pre-inspect your property
- This is the area of highest risk of the contract falling out due to issues found in inspections and the negotiation process
- Take the emotions out and focus on this as a business deal
- At this stage, you need to plan to negotiate and grant concessions to the Buyer in order to close the deal
- Have your agent help manage the process; be patient as there is usually a lot of back and forth negotiating during this time
- Know in advance that this is one of the more stressful periods for both the Buyers and Sellers
- Focus on win-win strategies

ALWAYS REMEMBER - IT'S A BUSINESS DEAL

The majority of deals fall through during this stage. While having your house under contract with a Buyer, remember it's not a done deal until it closes. There may be delays, negotiations, and unexpected situations along the way. Keep your emotions out of it and focus on the business deal.

NO HOME IS PERFECT - EXPECT FINDINGS

It is important to note that no home is perfect and as you go through the process, you need to be ready to address any issues that arise. The findings will hopefully be minimal if you have gone through the process of the pre-inspection, as well as following through with our recommendations to get the property listed (such as minor renovations) and to get the house ready for the beauty competition. While going through the process, you should have identified the majority of issues. Regardless of any issue that may arise, the true objective of the previous steps is to eliminate surprises and prepare you to go through the appraisal and inspection process with minimal stress and anxiety. The objective is to minimize the findings and make the process smooth for both the Buyer and yourself. Being prepared will help you successfully tackle whatever findings may be revealed through the appraisal and inspection process. It will also prepare you for the unexpected.

IMPORTANCE OF THE APPRAISAL AND INSPECTIONS

In our experience the appraisal and home inspection processes are the areas where most of the contracts fall through.

If the appraisal is below the offer price, and you're not willing to reduce the price, odds are high that the Buyer will walk away from the deal. If the inspections discover issues that you and the Buyer cannot agree on how to address, the odds are also high that the Buyer, or yourself, will walk away from the deal.

When the reports come back, that will be the start of the negotiation process. In the early chapters of this book, we talked about how to build your team. One of the team members we recommended that you have ready and on standby is a general contractor. Your general contractor should be familiar with your pre-inspection report, should be on your side, and should be ready and willing to help you put your response together based on the findings.

Try not to stress out when you receive either the appraisal or inspection report. These are a necessary part of most real estate transactions. Be ready to deal and address the issues that may arise in them. It has been our experience that Buyers expect to gain from the inspection process. What we mean by this is that during this phase, Buyers expect you to either fix the issues that come up, provide price reductions to compensate for findings, or provide closing cost coverage. This is also why we have indicated that when you set your selling price, you need to leave room for negotiations on the offer price itself, for findings that may come up in these reports.

For one of the properties we were selling, the Buyer put in an offer that was $10K below the list price. We expected a lower offer since we were selling a house in a Buyer's market, so we priced the house accordingly. We informed our agent that we would accept the offer on the condition that the Buyer will not nitpick the inspection reports since we were giving a $10K concession on the offer price. After the inspection, even though no issues were found with either the roof or heating system, the Buyer came back and asked for an extra $8K concession since the roof was over 15 years old and the heating system was 10+ years old. The reasoning was that the Buyer was going to retire in the house and did not want to address the issues in the future. If we would not agree, it was going to be a deal breaker. In the end, we ended up walking away from the deal. This was one of the lessons learned that we talk about in this book. While it is important to leave room for negotiations, it is also important to know when, as the Seller, to walk away from a deal. We have learned that the probability of the Buyer asking for some kind of concession after the inspection reports is very high unless we get things in writing.

THE APPRAISAL

Banks and Sellers need to ensure that the offer price for the property is in the true market pricing range. A home appraisal is the process used where a professional appraiser, typically hired by the lender, provides an unbiased estimate of the true (or fair market) value of what the home is worth. The lenders order an appraisal during the mortgage loan process to assess the home's market value and ensure that the amount of money requested by the Buyer is in line with the loan-to-value amount of the loan the Buyer has applied for. This value can be from 65-100%, depending on the loan product, but most are 80%. The appraisal process typically includes recent sales information for similar properties. They also take into account the current condition and location of the property.

At this point in the process of selling your house, we believe you have followed our recommendation to get the property ready. This should help with the appraisal value of the property. If you have made a lot of improvements and repairs to the property over the years, keep records of the dates and costs, you should definitely mention these renovations to the appraiser. A new roof, siding, deck, or addition, as well as other improvements that you have made, can significantly increase the value of your home. Most appraisers will ask during their walk-through inspection, but don't assume they will know what to ask. Instead, itemize your improvements and have the list ready to share with the appraiser. We also recommend that you have your neighborhood binder that showcases your property available for the appraiser. Although they are licensed and certified, some appraisers can be assigned to appraise a home that is outside of an area they are familiar with. Again, don't assume they know.

TYPES OF HOME INSPECTIONS

Your real estate agent can provide an overview of the different types of inspections that Buyers typically ask for in your area. Here are the more common inspections:

- **General home inspection** - The whole home will be inspected to make sure it is all in good working order. This includes the roof, foundation, plumbing, electrical system, and just about everything else that makes a house a home.
- **Radon** - Radon is a radioactive material that can be distributed in the soil below and surrounding a home. If the concentration is strong enough, the radon can pose a health hazard to the inhabitants of the home.
- **Pests/Insects/Termites** - This inspection checks for termites, bugs, mice, or ant problems. It is good to show that you have a pest maintenance program as part of the regular maintenance to your home.
- **Well water, if not public** - If your house uses well water, then you should expect the Buyer will want to perform an inspection.

- **Septic System, if not public** - If not public, the septic tank will be checked. It is best to know what size your septic system is beforehand. Also, if you haven't had your septic tank pumped in quite a while, it is advisable that you do so before listing your home.

WHAT IS A HOME INSPECTION AND WHAT HAPPENS DURING IT

A typical home inspection takes a few hours for an average-sized house. Then the report takes a few additional days to complete. When the market is slow, it can be as quick as 3-4 days to get the report, but when the market is experiencing a surge, as in a Seller's market, the home inspection can take longer to complete.

During the inspection, the home inspector will go through the interior and exterior of the house to record any issues with it. Some of the items that home inspectors typically look for include:

- Water Damage
- Structural Issues
- Old/Damaged Roof
- Damaged Electrical System
- Plumbing Problems
- Insect and Pest Infestation
- Issues with the HVAC System

Home inspectors are not concerned with anything cosmetic in a home, unless it poses a potential safety issue.

HOW HOME INSPECTIONS AFFECT THE SALE

After the home inspection, the Buyer and Seller can either negotiate the contract or part ways completely.

- **Buyer walks away after the home inspection** - You will have to put the house back on the market or pull the house off the market. A lot of time and effort went into the contract that fell through and now you have to start over. It is important, as we mentioned earlier, to ensure that the contract clause does not allow the Buyer to just walk away if issues are found. Rather, the contract should provide and encourage the option to negotiate and mutually agree on ways to remedy the issues.
- **Negotiation over the home inspection (best scenario)** Depending on the terms of the contract between you and the Buyer, the Buyer may either request the Seller do the necessary repairs or request a credit from the Seller so the Buyer can do the repairs themselves. You can negotiate at that stage and hopefully reach an agreement to move forward.

PLAN FOR ISSUES; HAVE CONTRACTOR READY TO ADDRESS AND VERIFY FINDINGS

In our experience, the only way to negotiate on findings is if you are ready ahead of time to address them. You cannot take the findings personally. The Buyer is going through the normal motions of negotiations when presenting the findings. As part of the process, the results of the inspection are presented to you, and action, in most cases, will be requested if findings are found. When Sellers are not ready to respond to the findings, it is always a rush to find the right professionals to verify the findings and provide estimates.

Typically, you as the Seller will have a short window to respond to the findings. Locating and retaining last-minute professionals is a challenge. Having someone lined up in advance will help in keeping the Buyer interested. Time, at this point, is of the essence.

Over the years we have learned to have at least one or two general contractors ready to respond to the findings. Buyers will typically want to see more than one estimate for the cost to repair whatever is found through the inspection. If you do not agree with some of the findings in the home inspection, have your contractor(s) help you in responding as to why you don't agree with those particular finding(s). For instance, if the inspector thinks the roof won't last for another 5 years and suggests that it needs replacement, but it isn't that old and you really believe it has more life to it, have your contractor look at the roof and then respond to the issue in writing with their professional opinion.

THE WIN-WIN STRATEGY - DEALING WITH THE FINDINGS

We have learned the hard way, that if you do not plan upfront to provide some concessions, and have planned in your budget for this, the risk of the deal falling through is high.

We always believe that you need to plan for a win-win strategy. You need to come to a position during the negotiations that both parties believe they are receiving a good/fair deal. You may have to make additional concessions for the deal to move forward, but it is how you frame your position that may make the difference (this goes back to the experience of your sales agent in negotiations).

The negotiation strategy and options will vary depending on the situation. An experienced real estate agent can help you navigate through your options in this critical area.

THE TWENTY-FOUR HOUR RULE

One of our simple rules is that we give ourselves time to ensure that we are making the right decision and have thoroughly thought it through. Regardless of how good the deal looks, or whatever reason someone gives us as to why we need to sign now, our position has always been that we do not sign anything unless we sleep on it for one day. If the Buyer agrees to your terms and all that is needed is for you to accept, that is a decision that has already been thought through; however, if you have other terms to consider, we recommend that you take the time to formulate your position. Give yourself 24 hours.

GENERAL NEGOTIATION TIPS

GENERAL NEGOTIATION CONSIDERATION	DETAILS
LOOSE LIPS SINK SHIPS (KNOW THE IMPORTANCE OF SILENCE)	Only share information that needs to be shared. You will never know how people interpret information and how they react to it. In the same way you try to understand the Buyer's motivation, they might be doing the same to you, (i.e,. trying to understand your budget, your motivation to sell, how much lower they could go on their offer).
YOU GET MORE FLIES WITH HONEY —ANGER AND YELLING DO NOT RESOLVE ISSUES	Always deal with issues from a business point of view. You will be in situations in which you are furious; our recommendation is to deal with the situation in a calm and easy manner. By talking through the issues, you will get further in achieving your goal of selling your house. If you are upset, step away to allow time to think through the options.

GENERAL NEGOTIATION CONSIDERATION	DETAILS
DON'T UNDERESTIMATE THE STRENGTH OF RELATIONSHIPS, RESEARCH AND NETWORKING	Reaching out to your connections to ask questions and leaning on experts for advice will help you in your negotiations.
EVERYTHING IS NEGOTIABLE; YOU JUST NEED TO ASK	At times people tell us that we should not ask for certain things, because things are done a certain way in this industry, or that something is impossible and to not even try for it. There may be situations when you are not sure if you can negotiate a point. Keep in mind that you are doing this for the future of your family. If you think you can negotiate something, all you need to do is ask!
FRAMING AND EXPANDING THE PIE	If we learned one critical thing from our MBA classes, it is that how you present the issue will make a huge difference in the end. Once you understand the position that you would like to achieve, always think on how best to present it so that it makes sense or is attractive to the other party.
KEEP IT SIMPLE AND ASK LEADING QUESTIONS	When you are not sure of the exact position of the other party, try to ask the right questions to get the answers you need before you make a decision.

COUPLES' ACTION SUMMARY

As we enter this inspection and appraisal phase of selling our house, we are very aware of the risks associated with this phase. We always strive to understand the needs of our Buyers through this stage and see what options we have to keep everything moving forward.

1. Plan ahead for issues that could arise during this stage.
2. Have an action plan for dealing with possible negotiations as issues arise.
3. Have contractors ready for any repairs that may need to be completed prior to the closing.
4. Make sure to get confirmation of Buyer's mortgage approval (if applicable) on or before the date it is required and specified in the contract.
5. If it looks like closing is going to be delayed due to any repairs or other issues to work through, make sure the closing will not go past the date specified in the sales contract. If it will be past that date, make sure an addendum to the contract specifying the new closing date is signed by all parties.
6. Follow the Twenty-Four Hour Rule.
7. Don't be afraid to ask questions.
8. Present issues in a positive way; be open minded and cooperative, but expect the same from the Buyer.

This is a time when you will need to work even closer as a team. Our experience has shown us that during this period of the process is when we have to work with each other to find a solution that we both agree on. At times we do not fully agree, but it is important that when issues arise, we look for a middle ground, knowing that down the road we have a whole new phase of our lives.

NOTES

TASKS

The Close, the Move, and Final Thoughts

Time To Celebrate

The closing process is the final step in selling your home.

All the hard work you have put through to sell your house is about to reach its objective.

You need to understand your closing costs since they will dictate how much money will be provided to you at the close of the deal.

You need to be prepared for the final walk-through and be ready to vacate the house by the closing date.

Finalize Your Move

- *Notify utilities.*
- *Set up mail forwarding.*
- *Cancel any home insurance policies as of the closing date.*
- *Contact your financial institutions and update them with your new address.*
- *Contact your auto insurance company and inform them of the address change. If moving across states, understand that your rates may change or you may need to look for a new insurance carrier.*
- *Cancel any monthly service fees. These can include items such as home alarm, HVAC maintenance contracts, pest control, and/or garden maintenance fees.*
- *Notify family and friends of your new address.*

CHAPTER FIFTEEN

THE CLOSE, THE MOVE, AND FINAL THOUGHTS

You have made it through the inspection phases, and now you're on your way to the closing table. Make sure you understand the final steps and what is needed to finalize the close, and prepare your move.

- The closing process is the final step of selling your house
- All the hard work you have put in to sell your house is about to reach its objective
- You need to understand your closing costs since they will dictate how much money will be provided to you at the close of the deal
- You need to be ready for the final walk-through and to vacate the house by the closing date
- Gather extra keys, garage door openers, etc. that the Buyer will need
- Remember, it's not a done deal until all documents are signed and the sale is recorded
- If you have a question about anything at the closing, be sure to ask; if you decided to leverage a licensed agent, they can help you quickly answer the questions that you may have
- Be happy for the Buyer(s), and happy for yourself. A new stage in your life is about to begin!

KNOW WHAT TO BRING TO CLOSING

Items such as a photo ID are required at the closing, because the closing agent will need to identify you even if they know who you are. Check with your agent to ensure you have a list of any other items that are needed.

THE CLOSING - LAST STEP IN SELLING YOUR HOUSE

Closing is typically the last phase in the home selling process. This is when the final documents are signed, and the money is exchanged in order to transfer ownership of the property to the Buyer. Additionally, it is the time when the real estate agent is paid his/her commission. Other costs, such as remaining taxes, water, electric bills, and closing attorney's fees, are also paid.

The closing date is the date ownership of the property is officially transferred from the Seller to the Buyer. In addition, during this process, you as the Seller will pay off any loans/mortgages that are owed on the property. As a Seller, you also need to work hard to ensure you are ready to vacate the house and all your belongings in advance of the closing unless otherwise agreed in writing.

As a Seller, one of the important documents that you must be sure to review and understand is typically called "The Seller's Closing Statement" or the "Settlement Statement." This statement provides an itemized list (detailed breakdown) of costs (fees) and money owed to you (credits). The statement will show the funds that you will be receiving (net profits) as the Seller. In addition it summarizes the finances of the entire transaction.

Closing is typically handled by an escrow/law firm, whose job is to protect both you and the Buyer by ensuring that all money, documents, and other items needed to close the sale are properly exchanged.

In summary:

- The closing process is everything that happens from when you accept an offer until the date of closing. When completed, the ownership of your house is officially transferred to the Buyer.
- Closing costs can add up. Many of the costs that you'll incur as the house Seller will be deducted from your proceeds from the sale and included as part of your closing costs.
- The amount of equity that you have in the house, as well as the offer price and additional costs, will dictate the amount of money that will be given to you at the end of the transaction.

FINAL WALK-THROUGH

- The final walk-through typically occurs 24 hours before closing, although it can also happen on the day of closing, prior to the closing meeting. The Buyer and their Buyer agent will walk through the property one last time to make sure everything is still as expected and as agreed upon. They will check that all required repairs have been made, that the property is clean, and that all of your belongings have been removed unless you've arranged for certain items to stay. If the Buyer discovers any issues, you'll need to address it or the closing might be delayed.

HIGH LEVEL SUMMARY OF CLOSING COST

- It is important to understand all the costs that are associated with the closing since closing costs will be taken away from your final accepted offer. Simply put:

Accepted Offer - Closing Costs = Money you get to take home

Closing costs will vary depending on the terms of the specific transaction and the terms/agreements that you have negotiated with the Buyer. Your agent and/or your lawyer/settlement agent will be able to walk you through all the different costs that are listed in the settlement statement. In general, typical costs include:

- Mortgage payoff / prepayment penalty
- Additional Loans
- Real Estate agent commission fees
- Title Search and Insurance
- Settlement or attorney fee
- Taxes (owed and transfer)
- Utility Bills (final bills based on transfer)
- Recording Fees
- Closing credits to the Buyer (depending on your contract agreement)
- Preparation of Deed (Seller's responsibility)
- Other fees for costs associated with the sale of your house

THE MOVE

As you have a lot on your mind at the time of the close and the move, it's helpful to have a simple checklist to follow in your final planning. This checklist can include the following:

- Notify Utilities
- Notify cable/internet company
- Change of address with post office, set up mail forwarding
- Change of address with friends, family, publications, and others, as appropriate
- Cancel any home insurance policies as of the closing date
- Contact your financial institutions and update with your new address
- Contact your auto insurance company and inform them of the address change, if moving across states, rates may change or you may need to look for a new insurance carrier
- Cancel monthly service fees. These can include things such as home alarm, HVAC maintenance contracts, pest control, and garden maintenance fees

ONLINE RESOURCES

With today's online searches, a lot of additional information exists to help you plan and be prepared for selling and closing on your home. The intention of this book is to provide a baseline and roadmap on a wide range of topics. If you're looking for more information, we provide some key search terms in different areas to help you on your journey. You can use our book as a baseline and expand on the specific areas of focus.

Additionally you can visit us online at this website::

TheHappyCouplesGuide.com

Our goal is to provide online resources and information in support of your life journey.

ADDITIONAL CONSIDERATIONS

In looking back at our experiences and the different challenges that we have gone through as part of our investments, as well as our personal home moves, we know that we have not covered every scenario in this book. Our hope is that we have provided you with a baseline based on our experience to help you kickstart your journey and to make it easier. Some other consideration that we recommend you consider and plan around, if applicable to you, include:

- Relocation considerations
- Selling and buying at the same time
- House is not selling and has been on the market for an extended time
- You have pets in the house
- You're selling a rental unit rather than your house
- You're not happy with your real estate agent
- You decide you need to pull your house off the market

COUPLES' ACTION SUMMARY

Once you have reached the closing stage, and if you have followed our approach and recommendations, hopefully you will be ready to celebrate. Here are some things to remember on or just prior to closing on the home:

1. Review all closing statements; ask questions if you do not understand something; Federal rules require you to receive these closing documents for review at least three days prior to closing
2. Make sure you have notified utility company, cable company, fuel delivery, and any other services of the date you are moving and will be stopping service with them
3. Don't be surprised if you get emotional about leaving the home you are closing on—this is normal
4. Go through a checklist for all the final details you need to address prior to the closing
5. Make sure everything is clean and in order for the walk-through prior to the closing
6. Be sure to give the Buyer house keys, garage door openers, etc., that need to be left with the new owners
7. If your listing agent did a great job for you, consider giving them a good review and make sure you have a few of their cards to pass out to others thinking of selling or buying a home in the area
8. Now, go and celebrate! You've accomplished selling your home successfully and a new adventure awaits you!

You will have to work hard to get to this stage. We hope that our experience and the information provided in this book will help you and your family develop an action plan to make the whole process easier.

FINAL THOUGHTS

We truly believe that with proper planning and an understanding of the market, as well as understanding the process and steps of listing and selling your house from beginning to end, you will be able to find a Buyer and transfer ownership in any market with assurance and the least amount of stress. It will take patience and hard work on your end, but with this understanding, you can persevere and see it through. It truly is not an easy process and will require time and effort and a lot of patience, but it can also be an exciting journey. We wish you all the best in selling your home, and in the new adventure that awaits you after you've done so.

We hope that by reading this book we have provided you with tips and approaches to make the selling process of your house easier. We wish you the best, and we hope that like us, your journey of selling your house puts you on the path to where you want to be for you and your family. May you succeed and achieve all that you plan and hope for. We leave you with an Irish blessing:

May the road rise up to meet you.
May the wind be always at your back.
May the sun shine warm upon your face,
and rains fall soft upon your fields.
And until we meet again,May God hold you in the palm of His hand.

NOTES

NOTES

TASKS

- [ ]
- [ ]
- [ ]
- [ ]
- [ ]
- [ ]
- [ ]
- [ ]
- [ ]

ABOUT THE HAPPY COUPLES GUIDES

The Happy Couples Guide (TheHappyCouplesGuide.com) series is designed to provide a practical, comprehensive guide that can be easily implemented by working individuals, especially couples who are both working. The series is designed to provide insight and lessons learned from other couples.

The Happy Couples Guide concept is creating books and stories that are motivational and geared toward taking life lessons and providing the mechanisms to share these life stories and experiences with others. The series is intended to share with you how couples can leverage each other's strengths and divide up roles and responsibilities to make it work.

As we move forward and take the series to the next level, we hope to bring forth exciting titles that focus on original content in all formats with the mission to educate, entertain, and inspire readers for generations.

May we recommend you get a copy of our books for each one of you; the book is designed such that you can track your notes and tasks at the end of each chapter. The book can be utilized as a planning guide to capture your notes and tasks as you read through the series, ultimately helping you build a better future for you and your family.

If you enjoyed this book, we hope you'll take the time to take a look at some of the other great books from the Happy Couples Guides

The Happy Couples Guide to Investing in Rental Property details the story of a hard working, middle class couple who tried different areas of investment before turning their attention to rental properties. With volatility in stock markets, 401Ks, and other investments, their strategy has been to focus on real estate in rural areas, in order to build wealth and generate a source of continuous passive income.

The Happy Couples Guide to Buying Your First Home is designed for reading early in the home buying process, even prior to engaging with a real estate agent, and to refer to again and again. Planning and buying your home can be an extremely stressful and challenging process. This guide will help you define your family needs, provide an easy-to-follow process, highlight the Pros and Cons of using a real estate agent, present recommendations and interview questions for choosing an agent, and compile negotiation strategies to help you throughout the buying process.

The Happy Couples Guide to Planning Your Child's College Admission Process empowers parents and caregivers in getting a head start in supporting, and planning their child's college admissions process from early childhood to high school. Designed as a workbook, it can be personalized for your child allowing you to capture information over the years that will be needed as part of the application process.

The book is divided into four sections to support you and your child through this journey: Getting Ready, Components of a Successful Admissions Application, Financing, and a Bonus Section with information on how a working couple can save money to support their children's education.

The Happy Couples Guide to Homemade Cheeses & Yogurt provides simple and easy to follow recipes that you can use in your own kitchen to make fresh cheeses and yogurt for your family. Over the years, we have enjoyed yogurt and cheese produced by Jinan's dad, master cheese maker Ziad Jaber, who has a Master of Science degree in Animal Science and Dairy Production and had his own dairy farm. The process is straightforward. Once you master the basics steps, you can have fun and experiment with the process and varieties to create your own unique and flavorful cheeses and yogurts.

Made in the USA
Monee, IL
08 November 2026

67380778R00125